VOW TRIUMPH

BREAKING DOWN THE MARRIAGE VOWS

ANGELA E. ROLLE

Published by Love Inspiry LLC

www.loveinspiry.com

The characters and stories in this book are based on a true experience from the writer and her husband's marriage. Any similarity to any other persons, living or dead, is coincidental and not intended by the author.

Unless otherwise noted, all scripture quotations are taken from the King James Version Bible.

Book design by Angela E. Rolle via Canva

Printed in the United States by Lulu Enterprises, Inc.

ISBN: 978-0-578-51405-5

VOW
TRIUMPH

This book is dedicated to my grandmother, *Mary Alice Kitchen*. May your soul rest in heavenly peace.

I believe your humble spirit and servant leadership lives in me. You left me with the gift God gave you of serving others before yourself and walking instead of talking Christ-like. You have left an example for all your descendants, and I hope to continue to honor your legacy.

I love you.

Acknowledgements

The following people I am acknowledging are some who have encouraged me, helped me prosper mentally or financially, or kept me from walking off the ledge (wink!). I appreciate you all.

I first want to give honor to my Lord and Savior Christ Jesus. I sincerely thank God for everything. He is my source of strength, my guidance, and protection. Lord, I thank you for protecting my thoughts and insecurities. Thank you for shining your light on me and showing me positivity in you. Thank you for helping me appreciate everything I have instead of focusing on what I don't have. Thank you for instructing me that I can't do anything without you. Thank you for teaching me that everything will work out for my good in the end.

A special thank you to my husband, Elder Nathan E. Rolle for the constant encouragement and empowerment you give me. Your endless motivational moments and "pump up" sessions genuinely aid me. I am such a blessed woman to have a special man like you in my life. Through many ups and downs, good days and bad days, we have truly triumphed in our vows. I am forever grateful for that.

I thank the Lord that he placed you in my life nearly thirty-one years ago. I loved you then, and I love you now.

To my parents, Alfonso Tolliver Jr. and Michelle Mason, I love you both. You gave me life and good looks! I am genuinely thankful for both of you and your continued support. To the best stepparents in the world, Randall Mason and Vernisha Tolliver, thank you for supporting me and loving me like your own flesh and blood.

To my grandparents, Alfonso Tolliver Sr. and Vivian Tolliver, thank you for leading by example. If it weren't for your teachings, I wouldn't be the person I am today. Martha Peyton, my Granny Gran, my great-grandmother, I love you so much. You are full of life and wisdom. Your wisdom is something that I will hold on to for the rest of my life.

To my sisters and two little brothers, know that I always wanted to set an exceptional example for you to follow. Though I have made mistakes in my life, I hope you learn that no matter how many times you face a setback or fail, get back up, dust yourself off, and keep moving. I hope you learn to never give up on yourself and know that God is always near even when he seems far. I love you all so very much.

To my Father-in-law and Mother-in-law, Elder Larry Rolle and Bonita Rolle, I appreciate you accepting me into your life as a daughter. I am grateful for all the assistance you have provided us on days where everything was falling apart.

To my nephews, Derrick Kitchen-Dunlap, Jayden Howard, Kameron Tolliver, Benjamin Smith, and Kole Tolliver, your Auntie loves you little crazy boys. You all light up my world when I am around you.

A special thank you to my current supporters and new supporters I may gain. Every time I release content, understand that I pray it is of God and it will strengthen you, should you be going through a difficult time. My mission in life is not to be a big name, but to be the best of me I can be. When I am being myself, I can serve and inspire you in transparency and love!

God bless you all and may Heaven smile upon you.
–A.E.R

Contents

TRIUMPH ˈtrī-əm(p)f

a great victory or achievement.

synonyms: joy, accomplishment, success, attainment

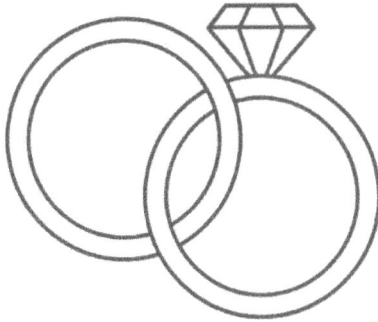

There is triumph in your vows.

Prelude

"Will you marry me?" The four words most girls dream about and the four words most men will prepare to say. Women dream about how they will be proposed to and how they will say yes. Men think about how they want to pop the question. *Am I going to throw a party with all her family and friends, or will it just be something more intimate?*

When the day of the proposal finally comes, we get incredibly excited. Then, we take engagement photos. Next, we spend six months to a year planning the wedding, or maybe you go to the justice of the peace. No matter what, for the most part, we all recite the same vows—the vows that will initiate a lifelong commitment to our significant other.

The reality is that many people don't know the meaning behind the vows they say, and the journey they really embark on. The fact is that many people don't take their vows seriously. The truth is that many people don't ever think about the worse, the unfortunate part that may come, and the sickness that could arrive.

It's reasonable to go into marriage optimistic of for better, for richer, and to remain healthy. Nevertheless, we must realize that in marriage challenges will come up, and those vows will be tested. The satisfaction comes in taking those challenges, working through them, making it to triumph, and strengthening the next couple.

You should not enter marriage lightly. Knowledge is power. I grew up in a two-grandparent household. My grandmother was an old-fashioned working wife, and my grandfather was a hardworking husband. I saw my version of how a marriage should be, what it entailed, and how a wife should treat her husband. As I entered my marriage, I emulated what I saw for eighteen years. That was my knowledge. It was my training to become the wife I am today, with my own little flare.

There are tools and resources out there to have a successful marriage. I know, firsthand, that marriage can be challenging and intimidating. After all, you are merging your single life with the life of another human being. Try doing that at eighteen! To be fruitful, you must think together, build together, talk through things, study other successful couples, and be able to manage adversity successfully. It can feel overwhelming, and that overwhelming feeling is valid.

The divorce rate in the United States is at an all-time high. If people knew what they were getting into and fully understood the vows they said, I am optimistic that the divorce rate would decline.

Sadly, people jump into marriage for all the wrong reasons. These reasons include children being involved, everyone else is doing it, pressure, status, and other perks. Marriage should be bonded by nothing else but pure love. When you are bonded by true love and not blinded by lust, you can say your vows with certainty and competence that you will make it until death do you part.

Vow Triumph is a guide full of stories and wisdom to help you navigate through your marriage vows and genuinely understand the meaning behind the promises you will make or have already made before your family, friends, and most importantly God. This guide will help you know that poor may come, sickness could happen, and worse will likely stumble upon you. No matter the magnitude, some type of adversity will be initiated in your marriage. The best part is this guide will show you the magic that happens when you stick around!

To Be My Wedded Husband

The husband is the leader, a protector, provider, and the man right under Christ. Husbands are the glue that keeps the family functioning and thriving—functioning with love, health, and financial stability. As the leader of the household, the husband sets the precedent of being Christ-like, ambitious, and fostering. Any good leader understands that they must put encouragement and empowerment into their followers to get something out of them. Like so, any good husband wants to see the success of their family. They thrive off seeing their family flourish and don't mind cultivating the garden to have beautiful flowers come out of it.

To be my wedded husband signifies that man shall join his wife in holy matrimony. There are responsibilities on the husband to keep the sanctity of the marriage blessed and a light to others. God designed marriage so beautifully and left us with some excellent instruction on how to successfully walk through life together as one flesh. Some of the responsibilities and commandments for a husband to successfully love his wife according to the Bible are:

- "Husbands, love your wives, even as Christ also loved the church, and gave himself for it;" (Ephesians 5:25 KJV).
- "Likewise, ye husbands, dwell with them according to knowledge, giving honour unto the wife, as unto the weaker vessel, and as being heirs together of the grace of life; that your prayers be not hindered" (1 Peter 3:7 KJV).
- "Husbands, love your wives, and be not bitter against them" (Colossians 3:19 KJV).
- "So ought men to love their wives as their own bodies. He that loveth his wife loveth himself" (Ephesians 5:28 KJV).
- "For this cause shall a man leave his father and mother, and cleave to his wife; And they twain shall be one flesh; so then they are no more twain, but one flesh" (Mark 10:7-8 KJV).

- "For the husband is the head of the wife, even as Christ is the head of the church: and he is the savior of the body" (Ephesians 5:23 KJV).
- "But he that is married careth for the things that are of the world, how he may please his wife" (1 Corinthians 7:33 KJV).
- "And Adam said, This is now bone of my bones, and flesh of my flesh: she shall be called Woman, because she was taken out of Man" (Genesis 2:23 KJV).
- Husbands, you were designed to be faithful to your wife and stay away from women that will provoke the purity of your marriage (Summarized from Proverbs 5).

What are some qualities you think are necessary to be an effective husband?

The Bible goes into great length about the role of a husband. The husband, as head of household, has an important task. The tension that a man faces every single day to be a good husband should not be overlooked. It's an enormous responsibility to take care of the home. The same way we can get stressed on a job or stressed with life, in general, is the same way husbands can get stressed. Nevertheless, the husband should continue to possess certain qualities and characteristics that emulate Christ to lead his bride and future tribe effectively.

The greatest thing I love about my husband is his love for the Lord. He fears the Lord, respects the Lord, reads his Bible every single day, and most importantly he is a doer of the word. There is nothing more I admire about him than the way he seeks first the kingdom of God. With this, my fear of him as my leader in our home is nonexistent. Because he honors the Lord and knows where his help comes from, I have full confidence that he will make the best decisions as humanly possible.

My husband and I initially met in the church. *Go figure!* As little kids, we knew of each other, but we didn't honestly know each other. I always knew our relationship was heaven sent because I loved him before I even knew the true meaning of love. Before I could fully understand the definition and the feeling, I was feeling it. I used to chase him around the church, and he paid no attention to me. For the longest, I thought the love was not reciprocated.

As we grew older, I straggled away from chasing him around the church. We had a mutual understanding through unspoken intimacy that we were meant to be. We never had to say a word to each other. I remember one time explicitly we were passing through a small narrow hallway at church. We had on the same color green. It was around the time "Talkin' To Me" by Amerie came out and I felt all the words to her song.

We locked eyes, and there was a common understanding right then and there that sooner or later we would be together for real. There was an understanding and confirmation that both of us had that day to where he knew I loved him, and I knew he loved me. A year later we started our journey together, and a couple of years after that, we were married.

My husband doesn't like to talk about himself and just how wonderful of a husband he is. He believes there is always room for improvement and growth—which there is, but that's with anything! He won't tell you how he provides my needs and wants, cuddles me, kisses me gently on the forehead, works every single day to offer a great life for me, and so on. He believes that is what a man is supposed to do. As a Christian, he understands his role as a husband. He is an example and a role model.

Husbands were designed to love their wife as Christ loved the church. This means the love a man has for his wife should be unconditional, authentic, and eternal. You will never find anybody on Earth that is perfect, but you will find the one that is perfect for you. When you find the person that is solely meant for you and you intended for them, you will be able to love without condition. The flaws and faults of that person will be discounted.

Your love will be authentic and not forced. It won't be a plagiarized love concerned with material things, and what it appears to be as opposed to what it is. Your love will flow organically. When you find that person, it will be eternal. It will be until death do you part, and even after his or her death, you will still love that person.

What does Christ loving the church mean to you? How can it be exemplified in your relationship?

Sometimes when we are speaking to people, we will make a statement and then say "but." Anytime we make a statement, such as "I love you, but if you get sick I won't be able to handle it," we are dismissing everything we just said before that. The word "but" is a condition. Loving someone without condition is eliminating the "but" and replacing it with the statement "I love you, and if you get sick, I am going to take care of you." Loving without condition is longsuffering and reception of who a person is and what they can or can't offer you.

My husband, Nate, has loved me without condition. His love for me is real, and I genuinely believe he will still love me even if I leave the world before him. There is a certain feeling I get when I am around him, when he gives me advice, and when he hugs me. Maybe one day when I feel like a memoir is warranted, I will go into detail; but I remember having to divulge a big secret that only immediate family knew. It was something that happened to me when I was at the tender age of twelve. I remember telling him years down the line. His response wasn't doleful, but it was understanding. It wasn't something that I necessarily had to share with him, but he made me feel comfortable, and his unconditional love for me made me vulnerable enough to do so.

We all have heard of the saying, "real recognize real." It's one of the most accurate phrases used. The authenticity of your relationship should be confirmed in the way you talk, walk, and think. Your actions should match your thoughts, and your thoughts should match your actions. We are supposed to be a light to others as the scripture tells us that.

On the contrary, real can also recognize fake. The fake part is men marrying to cover up something about themselves, men marrying because they feel pressured whether by the woman or their community, women marrying because their clock is ticking, and women or men marrying for some other gain. The authenticity of your relationship requires connecting with your partner on a more profound level.

When there is no genuineness and truth in a relationship, the two parties will have a hard time connecting beyond a sexual experience. Having a genuine love is required to be successful. As a leader and having control over marriage, husbands should be able to recognize a real wife versus a wife who is wanting the benefits and the label. When trouble arises, or temptations sneak in like a serpent, if your relationship is not genuine, it won't sustain the pressures and forces that will work against you to try to bring you down.

Think about a disconnect you may have in your relationship. Ask yourself what the cause of the disconnect is and what can be done to connect on a stronger level.

Eternity is a time with no end. There should be no end or limits on love and marriage. Do you know how Christ loves us with an everlasting love? Since we should strive to be like Christ, we need to love our spouse with an eternal love—to infinity, till death do we part!

27

Think about a passion you have. Let's take basketball for example. Nate loves the game of basketball. He grew up playing it and played in high school. He came upon much adversity when he broke his leg playing the sport. He veered away from it, but still has a tremendous amount of love watching the game, and I'm pretty sure it will remain that way forever. The same way he still loves the sport of basketball even when adversity happened, is the same way we should love our spouse.

To love someone like Christ, our Heavenly Father, has loved the church is immense. Regardless of the adversity that Christ faced from being whipped all night long, having a crown of thorns on his head, among other things, he still loved us. He endured so much for us. No matter what comes up in the relationship, husbands should love their wives ceaselessly.

Respect is an essential aspect of the marriage vows. As women are the weaker vessels and the man is designed to lead the home, whatever husbands desire to see is what husbands should exemplify. It's like parents teaching their children. Do as I say not as I do is not practical. To be an active parent, it must be do as I do. Parents need to illustrate what they want their kids to demonstrate, and that happens with action. Respect consists of multiple things to include honoring marriage to the wife, supporting her endeavors, and valuing her opinion to name a few.

Respecting and honoring marriage includes being and acting like a husband when the wife is not around. It requires a husband to uphold the values that he was given by Christ to be faithful to one woman, his wife. Respect and honor require wanting to see the wife cultivate her dreams and aspirations. It entails helping the wife get to a high point in her life and keeping her there.

Have you ever heard of the phrase, "too many chiefs and not enough Indians?" This means there is too many bosses or leaders and not enough workers or followers. As a leader (chief) of anything, you must know when to be a follower (Indian).

My husband is the leader of our home, but I have specific skills that I'm more talented at than he is. I'm very good at creating budgets, organization, and establishing financial boundaries. As a leader, he utilizes me to be of help to him. Just because you use the Indian doesn't make you less of a chief. What it makes you is a resourceful chief.

Chief and Indian Exercise: what skill does the Indian have over the chief that can be used for the betterment of the relationship?

Men have reputations for being egotistical and overbearing. Because the Bible says the woman's desire should be to their husband, some men take this literally— even when they are weak in an area. A woman's desire should be to her husband, but a husband has the responsibility of utilizing his wife for good, as a help meet to better the family. *Take note that the Bible said, "desire should be to the husband."* It did not mention the boyfriend or the baby's father.

One thing about feeling love for someone is when it truly exuberates your body, it fills you up with the responsibility of protecting a person, shielding them and their feelings, being compassionate towards their imperfections, accepting them and their physical flaws, and treating them as you would treat yourself. You can't help but treat them with dignity and respect. You love them as Christ instructed a man to love his wife—as your own bodies. Loving someone as much as you love yourself can seem unrealistic until you fall in love.

During "Snowmageddon" in Atlanta, I was stranded in a neighborhood. I had slid down ice and couldn't get out. I was completely stuck, nervous, and cold. My husband walked nine miles in the dark and in the cold snowy weather to sit in the same unfriendly condition with me. He walked through the ice and snow so that I wouldn't be alone all night. Close to frostbite, he sacrificed his own body to get to me.

In your opinion, how can love be shown to signify loving your significant other as you love your own body?

My Public Speaking Instructor was teaching one day in class, and she utilized the term "intense fellowship." It was a term her Pastor used. I have since adopted the term because it's a nice way of saying, "argument!" One thing about arguments is that they will happen. It doesn't matter if they are small or big. They shouldn't happen often, but they will happen. Understand that intense discussions are healthy; however, consistent arguing is not healthy. I elaborate on this more in depth in my next book.

If you are an avid follower of mine on social media, you understand that I am big on knowing what you are fighting against. The devil desires to sift you as wheat (Luke 22:31 KJV). He desires to tear down your home. He desires that you live a miserable life. Just like the serpent he was in the garden beguiling Eve, he wishes that your marriage fails. He will come in the form of everything you want and lust after. When you know what you are fighting against, you know how to pray and what to pray for. You know the fight isn't against your significant other, but the devil.

As a leader, husbands need to know when to diffuse an argument that can be escalating to something else. Bitterness, envy, aggression, and jealousy are the common denominators for disputes. Most leaders know how to diffuse situations to keep from escalating to the point of no return.

Think about leadership on your job. You may have a dispute with a coworker. It is leadership's job to diffuse the situation and bring it to resolution. This is precisely how the husband, the leader, should look at "intense moments of fellowship." Don't build your house on tit for tat or spitefulness. Husbands, your job is to establish grounds and the basis of the home.

The husband is head of the household. Being the head of a household comes with high accountability and obligation to the wife and future children. One thing about being the head of something or the leader, you must be a good follower. Moreover, in the husband's case, he needs to be a good follower of Christ. When following Christ and his direction, you can't go wrong. The same way you take care of your body by going to the gym and eating healthy is the same way you should nurture and care for your wife.

Ask yourself how you as a husband can better follow Christ and as a wife, ask yourself how your husband can better follow Christ.

Reflection Notes

_____

_____

_____

_____

_____

_____

_____

_____

_____

_____

_____

_____

_____

_____

_____

_____

_____

_____

To Be My Wedded Wife

The wife is the matriarch of the family. The person who clothes you, nurtures and protects you, becomes a shoulder to cry on, and the one that will do all the dirty work behind you. She is the woman right behind the husband operating in high strength to make sure the family is well taken care of on the opposite side of the man. She is the other half picking up the slack, duties, and responsibilities that nobody else wants to do.

To be my wedded wife means that woman shall join her man in holy matrimony. There are responsibilities on the wife to keep the sacredness of their marriage holy and a light to others. God designed marriage so beautifully and left us with some excellent instruction on how to successfully walk through life together as one flesh. The responsibilities of a wife to successfully love her husband according to the Bible are:

- "Wives, submit yourselves unto your own husbands, as unto the Lord" (Ephesians 5:22 KJV).

- "Unto the woman he said, I will greatly multiply thy sorrow and thy conception; in sorrow thou shalt bring forth children; and thy desire shall be to thy husband, and he shall rule over thee" (Genesis 3:16 KJV).

- "Who can find a virtuous woman? for her price is far above rubies" (Proverbs 31:10 KJV).

- "And the Lord God said, It is not good that the man should be alone: I will make him an help meet for him" (Genesis 2:18 KJV).

- "Now concerning the things whereof ye wrote unto me: It is good for a man not to touch a woman. Nevertheless, to avoid fornication, let every man have his own wife, and let every woman have her own husband. Let the husband render unto the wife due to benevolence: and likewise also the wife unto the husband. The wife hath not power of her own body, but the husband; and likewise also the husband hath not power of his own body, but the wife. Defraud ye not one the other, except it be with consent for a time, that ye may give yourselves to fasting and prayer; and come together again, that

Satan tempt you not for your incontinency" (1
Corinthians 7:1-5 KJV).

- "A virtuous woman is a crown to her husband: but
  she that maketh ashamed is as rottenness in his
  bones" (Proverbs 12:4 KJV).

- "She openeth her mouth with wisdom; and in her
  tongue is the law of kindness" (Proverbs 31:26 KJV).

- "That they may teach the young women to be sober,
  to love their husbands, that the word of God be not
  blasphemed" (Titus 2:4 KJV).

- "Every wise woman buildeth her house: but the
  foolish plucketh it down with her hands" (Proverbs
  14:1 KJV).

***What are some qualities you think are necessary to
become an effective wife?***

So, you're going to be a wife, or maybe you are already a
wife? Perhaps you are a man looking to find what a good
wife entails. If you look at the Bible and you read it

carefully, it may appear to be harsh towards the woman, her obligations, and how women are to conduct themselves.

Some women don't want to submit, some women don't want to be on the back burner, or we have some women who want to do everything for their husbands. We first must look at why women were designed, and that is because it is not suitable for man to be alone (Genesis 2:18 KJV).

Women were designed to be a companion to the man. Now, that doesn't give the man the right to treat a woman like rubbish; because as we previously discussed the husband is supposed to love their wives as Christ loved the church.

Do you think that the Bible is harsh on women and their role as a wife? Do you think your opinion is due to a lack of understanding or lack of compliance?

Just like the husband, the wife needs specific characteristics and traits to be successful. Men should be watchful of women who are haughty, contentious, and wild. Women should strive to be the best version of them according to the Bible. This includes working on yourself before entering a relationship, knowing who you are and what you stand for, believing in Christ, and trusting Christ that he will guide you in the right direction.

Women can be very fragile in emotions and character and easily persuaded when love is discovered. Engulfed with that tingly sensation of butterflies, a better judgment can be clouded. An essential attribute a woman needs before entering any relationship is self-worth.

Self-worth includes satisfaction with yourself, respect for your body, and pure happiness from within. It requires loving the inner person and what the inner person has to offer. It's not what a woman looks like that defines her, but how she permeates a room with her spirit. When a woman wholeheartedly loves herself, she won't withstand some of the hardships that most women allow themselves to endure.

Finding self-worth, self-love, self-esteem, and self-gratification will benefit the relationship and marriage in so many ways. When a woman understands herself, she understands the composition of relationships and how to navigate effectively to keep relationships healthy and constructive. A woman who knows her ambitions, who has goals, and wants a bright future will plan accordingly for the upcoming. This woman won't be afraid to discuss the logistics of life, such as where to live, how many kids, and financial plans and boundaries. She has desires for the future and doesn't want to waste time with someone who doesn't.

Pick an area where your self-worth can be increased. Is it causing a hindrance in the progression of your relationships? Write down three active steps in rectifying the problematic area.

Learning about wifely duties and becoming a great wife starts at home and takes training. Girls who don't see what a woman does for a husband generally have a hard time grasping the concept as opposed to girls who saw the example of a good wife. The case you have before you at home is what you will most likely try to emulate in your relationship. If a girl saw a toxic wife, she may become one herself. If a girl saw a toxic husband, she may attach more to a poisonous man as she matures. Thus, it's good to have a great example! If you don't have a good example, there are other ways explained in the introduction to educate yourself.

Every new year my goal is to become a better wife than the year before. It's what I strive to be—a great wife! I ask myself how I can be of better service to my husband. Although I had a great example of what a wife should be like, I feel as though I fall short from time to time. I feel as though I am not living according to how the Bible tells me I am supposed to live. Of course, I'm human. For me, something that I am so passionate about, I take seriously. I pride myself into doing the best job, according to the Lord. Let's talk about the role of a wife!

Submit to who? We are living in times where more and more women are becoming independent and not relying on men. Women don't want to submit themselves to anybody nowadays. Alternatively, they want to submit on their terms and stipulations. Back in the "good ole days," women stayed home, cooked, and cleaned. Women were to do as they were told, with no back talk.

Moreover, many women were physically and emotionally abused. Submitting to your husband is not that. It's not physical or emotional abuse. It's not being treated like a pawn or slave. Remember that the Bible tells the husband to love their wives as Christ loves the church. Christ didn't show abuse. Christ displayed love and concern for his people.

To fully submit to a husband, it is necessary to have a husband who is a follower of Christ and a doer of the word. Women have a hard time submitting to somebody who has no leadership, displays no love, no compromise, no compassion, no hope for the future, or men who have difficulties committing to one woman.

As a woman, choose the character of your partner and complete obedience to Christ and submitting to your husband won't pose a problem. When women start picking men with good looks, great jobs, and mundane things, the true essence of the person is missed.

Submitting to a husband can be hard if you are with someone who is not meant for you. Compatibility doesn't happen with every person that you meet. It is true that everyone who comes into your life is not expected to stay. It is true that some people are only meant to teach you lessons, which I am happy to say always turn into blessings. That is why it is essential to ask God for discernment and guidance when someone comes into your life. You won't be able to share a lasting commitment with just anyone. You may have a fleeting moment of feeling good, but there will be no longevity.

As a woman submitting to her husband, you should still have mental stamina. You shouldn't go along with ungodly behavior, you should still express your feelings, and you shouldn't be fearful of giving opinions on matters.

Actual submission is respecting and honoring your husband as the leader of your household. We are the weaker vessel. The Bible tells us this. Just as Christ is the head of your life and you follow him, so is your husband the head of the household and women should be able to willingly and earnestly follow the husband.

If I am transparent, I was very contentious as a young wife. It wasn't until I started reading my Bible thoroughly and learning from trial and error that I was doing everything wrong. I was and still am a domestic wife. What I lacked was a positive way of delivering conversation and opinions. In my head, I thought I was better at certain things than my husband was. I thought I had all the answers. I wasn't effectively communicating to him that there was a more excellent way of doing things. My conversation was abrasive and belittling. My behavior was unacceptable.

No matter what I did domestically, I wasn't fulfilling my full duty as a wife of respecting him as a leader. My last several jobs had terrible leadership and management. However, I didn't go on the job disrespecting them. So why would I have chosen to do that at home to my leader who was following Christ the best way he knew how.

As a woman, you may have a better way of completing tasks, budgeting, or whatever the case may be. The truth is, there are things that women are more efficient at than men. However, position yourself to be heard successfully with calmness and reasonable approach. Know that you chose a man who values what you have to say and wants to listen to what you have to say. Realize that aggression and being loud will not get you heard.

Don't be fearful of submission and think you become voiceless or irrelevant. Any good man will respect the opinions of whom he chose as a wife. When you study submission and when you are trying to understand what it means entirely, look at it as the golden rule. *Treat people how you want to be treated.*

Would you want a man to abrasively tell you that everything you do is wrong? Would you want a man to say to you that you don't know what you are doing? Would you want a man to make you feel like you are worthless and absurd? No! You would wish for a gentler approach. You would want someone to lift you and encourage you. As you wish to be treated with respect, you should reflect that in how you speak to your husband. The same respect the man was designed to give us is the same respect we should want to give him.

How can submission become active in your life? Where is submission lacking in your relationship?

In Proverbs 31:26 KJV it says, "she opens her mouth with wisdom and in her tongue is the law of kindness." Wisdom in the tongue knows what to say and what not to say, knowing when to say it and when not to say it. As we are taught in Ecclesiastes, there is a time for everything. There is our instruction clarifying us on what to do as a wife—to speak wisely, effectively, tenderheartedly.

When I became slowly in the word, I started learning this and most importantly started applying it. Application of what you know is more important than saying what you know. Studying our Bible is the only way we can learn to apply God's teaching and have effective marriages.

Proverbs 18:21 KJV says, "death and life are in the power of the tongue." Be careful and mindful of what you say because you can't take words back. This includes insults. I have said some demeaning things, and I've been on the receiving end. No matter how angry you get, words that hurt will stick around forever.

Speak life into your husband. If you see him weak in a particular area, give him an encouraging word. If he wants to be vulnerable, allow him the space to do so without making him feel feeble. Women, if you use your tongue for anything, use it for life and pray God strengthens the leader of your household.

Say a prayer for your husband or future husband that he becomes the best leader God designed him to be.

We often hear the scripture in the third chapter of Genesis indicating that because of the transgression in the garden, the desire of the wife is to be to the husband. There is so much in the word desire, such as faithfulness, love, and fostering. These are all the things a wife should desire to be to her husband. Desire is not a negative connotation, but a word of affection.

Read the third chapter of Genesis. What does desire mean to you?

Women should desire to be faithful to their husbands. Faithfulness is not something that should be challenging. It should come naturally. It shouldn't be something you try to do. When you love someone, you desire them and only them. You admire no one else but the person you are with— the person that is meant for you. The person that you marry should give you everything you need physically and emotionally. The person you marry should supply your earthly needs and wants. When you have to look elsewhere, you are trying to fill a void.

Think about if you ever looked on another man or woman and what you saw in them that sparked you. It grabbed your attention. Whatever sparked you in that other person is a void you feel in your relationship. If you were compatible with the person, nobody would ever be able to put a spark in you as your partner can. It's vital that your desire is to the right person. Majority of the times women spend years with the wrong man giving energy and life to the wrong person.

Withholding sex is something that the Bible speaks about very clearly. Have you ever been mad at your significant other and said, "I won't give him some" because of whatever reason? I have been there before trying to prove a point. Withholding sex can unintentionally hurt you. As sex is a natural part of married life, infidelity can be a leading cause by withholding it from your partner. Your job is not to punish the husband.

Women *should* desire to love and enjoy their husband. You shouldn't be compelled to love. That means you shouldn't be forced to love through pressure or the fact that children may be involved. When love is forced, and when love is pressured, your desire is to your complacency and not to the person. Your desire is to settling. With that, your desire can lead to unfaithfulness. It's similar to being in a prearranged marriage. I don't know about you, but I don't want to grow to love someone while already being married to them. I want the love to happen organically and affectionately *before* marriage.

Think about ways you can keep your desire to your husband.

Lastly, it would help if you desired to want to nurture your husband. It should make you feel good to care for your home. I remember my husband asking me what concoction

I use to make the clothes smell so good. I jokingly told him, "I can't tell you because then you won't need me." He said, "yeah right!" Still, I get great joy out of washing his clothes, making his dinner, making sure we have a clean house, and packing our clothes for travel. Nurturing is a part of being a wife and a mother.

The Proverbs 31 woman was a nurturer. She was a woman who was meant to do the man good and not evil. She was a woman clothed with strength and in dignity. She was a woman her children and husband idolized. She was a woman who spoke with wisdom and kindness. She was a woman of noble character. She was a woman who cared for and managed her household. She was a woman who feared the Lord. She was a woman that we should aspire to be in our talk and in our walk.

The Proverbs 31 woman was a help meet for her husband. The Bible teaches us that women were made from man and we were made because "it is not good for man to be alone." People typically associate a help meet as a companion, a partner, or a helper. While in modern day, that is fine to believe because women are companions and partners to their husbands. A help meet is a person suitable for you. It is someone that you can be equally yoked with. This woman described in Proverbs was ideal for her husband, and we know this because of how the husband and children felt about her and her actions.

Read about the Proverbs 31 woman. How do you as a wife or future wife emulate her? What did you learn from reading and where can you make changes?

Suitability requires connecting on a level with depth. It entails connecting spiritually and emotionally as anyone can connect physically. As a woman, you can go out right now and pick someone to have sex with, and they will gladly accept it. This level of suitability requires a more insightful level of thoughts, understanding, and awareness.

The primary requirement to prevent suitability issues is to select characteristic over materialistic. Women mess up terribly when choosing a man based on their financial stability. Financial stability is not a connection. There are tons of financially stable men, yet they are emotionally disconnected and spiritually unbalanced.

Women can be very demanding in needs and expectations. Sometimes a woman's expectation of a man is unrealistic. Yes, he is the leader. However, leaders make mistakes, leaders fall sometimes, leaders face setbacks, and most importantly leaders still need assistance. Being a wife who believes in her husband and the success of their relationship is paramount. A woman's expectation of her husband should match the energy and positivity that she puts into him.

List expectations you have of your husband or future husband. Now ask yourself are you matching his expectations and speaking life in him to be successful in those expectations.

A successful relationship takes two people understanding their individual roles. Your responsibilities as a wife are just as integral as the husband's responsibilities. Don't confuse submission and being the weaker vessel with unimportance. As described in Proverbs, your role as a wife is just as valuable. When a wife comprehends what she can do to be successful, she can easily obey and honor her vows with guarantee.

Reflection Notes

_____

_____
_____
_____
_____
_____
_____
_____
_____
_____
_____
_____
_____
_____
_____
_____
_____
_____

To Have & To Hold

———————————————————

I remember telling my husband the deepest darkest secret I was carrying around with me. It was a secret that only select people knew. I remember the day so vividly because of the nature of the conversation. He held the secret and never mentioned it again. He never brought it up in "intense moments of fellowship." He never brought it up in normal conversation. He accepted the secret and me. When you get married, you belong to each other. You won't be able to work through hardships without depending on one another. There are two primary ways this happens, and that's through accountability and support.

Having something or someone is possession and ownership. Pertaining to relationships, recognize that this is accountability. Think about jobs such as accountants, payroll clerks, customer service agents, or any positions who have accounts. These professionals are responsible for providing guidance, instruction, and handling all relevant matters. Typically, when something goes wrong with the account, the client will reach out to the professional to handle the case as they are accountable in rectifying the issue.

Once you enter the covenant of marriage, it is no longer about you and only you. You are now liable for your partner. Accountability in your relationship and for your partner consists of treating their feelings as your own, bearing their burdens, recognizing if you hurt them, being a good listener, communication, and possessing the appropriate qualities to implement this effectively.

What does being accountable to your partner mean to you?

Both parties have the responsibility to accept each other. Acceptance is being able to love a person beyond their faults and flaws. Beyond any secret they could ever tell you. Beyond any aggravation they may cause. Acceptance is being able to say no matter what you have to say to me; my love is bottomless. It runs deep enough to look past previous mistakes. This requires respecting one another's defects; because we all have them! If you are not willing to accept a person, you are not ready for the commitment of marriage.

Part of growing together is understanding that your partner's feelings now become your feelings. When they grieve, you grieve. When they are full of anguish, so are you. Mark 10:8 KJV says, "and they twain shall be one flesh: so then they are no more twain, but one flesh." Marriage is an intertwinement of two people forming to live as one, and living as one entails operating with acceptance of one another.

Love will hide a multitude of faults and flaws (1 Peter 4:8 KJV). Acceptance is birthed from compassion. Acceptance will be effortless and natural when the husband and wife have a genuine concern for one another. When you can understand why your spouse thinks the way they think or do the things they do, you are accepting them for who they are. Don't ever try to change a person but work with them in becoming a better them so you both can become a better us.

Pick one aspect of your partner that you wish you could change. Now, identify three ways you can be more accepting of your partner's behavior?

Accountability in your relationship also involves establishing your foundation. Appreciate that if you have the foundational principles in your relationship of Christ, friendship, and 100% honesty, you have acquired your good thing. Other than Christ, there is no better acquisition than to have found the person that genuinely loves you and that you genuinely love. There is nothing more significant you can have in life than to acquire the exact person meant for you. The person that you are meant to travel through life's ups and downs with. The person that is going to ride with you through thick and thin. When you have acquired that person, you have gained a lifetime friend and longevity will be longsuffering.

A strong foundation is what you will rely on when things aren't working out the way you feel it should. My foundation in my marriage first consisted of Christ. When things got rough for us financially, I released my fears and anxieties to Christ and was only looking to him for the answers. I solely depended on Christ to get us through those tough times. Christ would be right there throughout the journey letting us know he was with us.

One time we were at church and down to the last penny. We had traveled to church to worship the Lord, not knowing how we would get through the rest of the week. A man came up to my husband and wrote a $200 check out the clear blue sky and gave it to him. Talk about the power of God and his precious angels. Your foundation will be there to pick up the pieces when you have been shattered in calamity.

Individuals entering the commitment of marriage have the duty to keep their significant other from hurt. This doesn't just mean physically, but spiritually and emotionally. As a partner, it is your responsibility to be a shield to the complications your significant other may be faced with. This means keeping them away from people that will negatively impact your marriage. This means monitoring how you could offend your partner.

Unintentional hurt is not an excuse or a pass and is just as aggressive and upsetting as intentional hurt.

Since I married a preacher, I like to consider myself spiritually protected. Often when I hear certain preachers speak, I'm conflicted between what is being said. *Did they tell the story right? Do they have a clear perception of what the Bible was indicating?* I always ask my husband first. He gives me comprehensibility on what I heard. I love how I can ask any spiritual question, and as my brother in Christ, he is always willing to answer. He is willing to let me know if I misunderstood something, if I am reading too much into things, or if biblically it is wrong.

Accountability requires acknowledging wrongdoing even when it is unintentional.

Habitually, we look at relationships on outward appearance. The couple looks good, or they may be doing good things for people to see. We look at factors that are not trustworthy. We look at outward appearance and say, "relationship goals." Our relationship goals should be modeled after authenticity. It should be shaped after not how a couple looks, but how a couple carries themselves and how a couple honors their marriage vows. It should be modeled after how accepting the person is towards their spouse, how they value what they acquired through modest behavior, and how the couple keeps the commitment of marriage sacred.

List your top three non-materialistic relationship goals you have and a step by step plan to achieve those goals.

Accountability for your actions is indispensable. Relationships won't work unless two willing parties pledge to make it work. It starts with you! It begins by making sure that you are prepared individually to be liable for someone else. Are you ready to take on the role of lifetime friend, confidant, and soulmate? Are you prepared to be considerate of another person's feelings? Are you willing to stop entertaining people who aren't putting in good energy to your relationship? Are you ready?

When you recite the vow "to have," recite it with the mindset you will have strong feelings and concern for your spouse. Recite it with the intention of wanting to have an exceptional level of understanding. Recite it with the determination of loyalty to your spouse. Recite it with faith to have belief and trust in your spouse. Recite it with the utmost of integrity.

Sometimes when we are looking for comfort, we want to be held. I remember countless of times crying on the shoulder of my husband about personal things that have happened, not graduating from college at the "right time," and complaining about how much I hated my previous job. I can distinctively remember him holding me, almost like an infant because I was in real tears and just sad about my situation. He did what any great husband would do, be there physically to show me that he cares, and he is there for me.

Then there are times where we are looking for comfort in a different way. It doesn't have to be the comfort of being in the person's arms, but emotionally. There are many people not emotionally available. There are many people that can't deeply connect with you beyond the tangible. It's so vital that we marry someone willing to connect with us emotionally as sex will only satisfy a portion of your desires. Holding your spouse with care emotionally is depth in your relationship and is a genuine connection to the soul.

When you hold something or someone, you carry, or you support it. Carrying and supporting a person encompasses encouragement, empowerment, and inspiration. Note that just because you are supportive doesn't mean you agree and just because you don't agree doesn't mean you can't be supportive. Support is instituted by wanting your partner to know that you will be there for them regardless of the misfortunes that may arise.

There are times where your partner will need your support. It could be a job-related issue, a family matter, or a personal issue. Decisions will need to be made, and ideas will start to flourish in various situations. Your partner may want to do something against what you believe and what you don't agree with. You may think the situation is senseless and unjustified. However, part of being a supportive partner is knowing that your ways are not God's ways. It behooves us to show support because we don't know what God instructed our partner to do, no matter how erroneous we think it is.

Practice support by making yourself accessible to listen, give inspiring advice, and showing compassion.

When my husband and I were trying to recover from the financial struggle, things were still irregular for us. It takes zero seconds to fall into a trap, but years and years to get out of it. We were contemplating going back home to New Jersey and then put the plan in place to go back. Nate contacted his former manager who specifically told him that should something go wrong in Georgia; he always had a job waiting for him back home. Nate emailed and called the manager so many times, and he never responded. I was still ready to go because we would be around our family with more help and support than what was in Georgia.

Let me show you the power of God. The next day everything was catching up to Nate. He was feeling like a failure as a leader, husband, and provider. He had a church tape from his favorite preacher from 1983 and just so happened to be in a vehicle that had a tape player in it. He was feeling deficient on that day and God stopped by. His favorite preacher and a tape over thirty years old preached a message to him that will forever be in his heart. *Abide in the ship*! It was letting him know that although the winds may get contrary in your life, abide in the ship, abide in God's word, abide right where you are at, and soon the Lord will deliver you. My husband said that the tears just fell down his eyes.

God is so wonderful and always right on the mark. It was evident that God intended for him only to hear that message, which was at the needed time. He tried to listen to the tape the next day, and it wouldn't play. It is still a mystery, but God works like that. It's so crucial that you hear and know his voice. If you don't, you will miss the memo. Although your marriage may face threats, if you are rooted in Christ, he will give you clear direction.

Reflect on how God shielded and protected you from things you wanted but didn't get.

To my dismay, I was not happy about staying because God didn't deliver the message to me. Unfortunately, that's what was going through my mind. All I saw was what I wanted. He told him to abide, not me. I wanted to go back home, and I wanted to go right then and there. Sometimes God won't show you something, but he will show it through your partner.

This story is a prime example of why you need to be supportive regardless. If my husband had done what I wanted to back then, there is no telling where we would be. I thought peace was waiting for me on the other end. I thought I would be happy, but I don't know what could have been waiting back home for us. It could have been more turmoil and disappointments waiting on the other end. *Would I even have my company? Would I even be writing this book?*

Support is a fundamental part of your relationship. It would be best if you were your spouse's number one fan and most reliable support system. As a team, you shouldn't want to see your partner fail. Sometimes we can want to be right and say, "I told you so!" It would help if you wanted to see your partner win and encourage them to succeed in any way they can. It is mandatory for the success of your relationship that you support regardless of doubt.

In December of 2018, I graduated with my associate's degree in Business Management. The day after graduation I started applying for jobs. At this point, Love Inspiry LLC was up and running, I was podcasting, I was working on books, and just focusing on my business while filling out applications. I had over thirty applications out, and I was receiving denial after denial. Not one single person called me back. My husband looks at me and says, "I think you are doing what you are supposed to be doing."

Identify where you can be more supportive of your spouse.

Without his support, I wouldn't be able to maneuver how I want. I wouldn't be able to solely focus on getting my business up, working on my apparel store, working on my books, working on motivational speaking, continuing my education, or the podcast. Supporting your spouse through their dreams and aspirations, holding and lifting your spouse is empowerment and encouragement.

Everything won't go as planned in you or your partner's life. Their ideas may fall through and so will yours. This is where you carry them into their next endeavor. Please don't make them feel bad that things didn't work out but inspire your partner to move forward. Inspire your partner not to get weary on this journey called life. Inspire your partner to trust God that all things will work out for their good in the end.

If you are in the stage of good days, you will need to continue to support one another to make sure you stay there as long as possible. Pat your partner on the back from time to time and frequently compliment what they are doing well. This will make your partner feel valued and less frustrated. When you get in the stage of bad days, you will need to hold one another accountable to get out of that segment. Politely come up with a plan together to turn the negative into a positive. Ask what you can do to be of service. *Work together*!

These vows "to have and to hold" set a precedent for what's to come and what you will be required to do going forward. Moving forward you will have good days, and you will have bad days. You may be rich or poor. You may get sick or be as healthy as possible. You may feel like talking one day and the next day want to come home and go to sleep. Accountability for one another and support to one another will be compulsory to get through all this.

Exercise putting more positivity in your spouse than negativity. Give a compliment each day for a week of everything they are doing right.

Reflection Notes

_____

_____

_____

_____

_____

_____

_____

_____

_____

_____

_____

_____

_____

_____

_____

_____

_____

_____

From This Day Forward

What happens from this day forward? You commit. You agree and pledge to love and honor your spouse from this day forward. You commit to spending your life with this one person from this day forward. You commit to making things work even when it doesn't look good from this day forward. You commit to loving and cultivating your relationship from this day forward. You commit to be a loyal, consistent, and sincere husband or wife from this day forward.

Long before your wedding day you made a commitment to one another. You started dating, and then you committed to becoming boyfriend and girlfriend. You may have decided to move in together, which is another commitment. Then, you committed once you became engaged. You committed to a wedding date, you committed to planning it, and you committed to executing it.

***A commitment must take place until death. Consistently
pledge every day to be the best partner you can be.***

By the time you enter marriage, commitment should be
second nature. From this day forward is a promise. It is a
new commitment and covenant that you will make or have
made before God to remain husband and wife through thick
and thin, good or bad, and right or wrong.

The new commitment is your wedding vows. If you have
taken time to build on the foundation of your relationship,
you should know by now whether the obligation is
something that you see yourself doing with this person.

I committed at a very young age to get into a serious
relationship and to get married. I was a junior in high school
when my husband proposed. We had just come from a big
church meeting in July 2005. We left Philadelphia,
Pennsylvania and headed to the beach and boardwalk in
Atlantic City. He asked me to marry him on the sandy shore
of my hometown area and obviously I said yes!

Even being young, I've never had an issue committing to
my husband. I knew two things about our relationship; it

was meant to be, and I loved him beyond measure. From this day forward didn't start at the wedding, it started back in September 2003 when I was dragged to his car by the late Mack Johnson who had enough of us playing games. When I said my vows, it enhanced my commitment to him. My belief in our relationship and faith in God allowed me to love without condition and commit without a hoax.

One thing about committing to your spouse is that you must be dedicated to the person and the union. If you aren't dedicated, if you aren't all in, the relationship will be unsuccessful and ineffective. Dedication should be to your spouse and your spouse only. At this point, you have become one flesh. At this point, you have decided to put your spouse above mother, father, and everyone else. No other person should be placed before your spouse.

Aside from this being a new covenant and a more sacred promise, there is something else you should understand about from this day forward. On that beautiful day, you leave everything in the past. Let what happened in past years stay there. From this day forward shouldn't bring in old drama. In the heat of the moment, we can sometimes bring up old situations that have happened as if they are relevant to the current day. Drama from previous relationships or previous mishaps has no business in what you both have going on from this day forward. If you have to bring it up or it's a constant topic of conversation, reevaluate what is missing from your foundation or what is lacking from your relationship. It could be trust.

What in the past are you holding on to that can be a deterrent to your relationship progress? Challenge the relevancy to the present day.

Friendship is one of the most critical objectives in establishing a healthy relationship and a strong marital foundation. Think about elementary school, middle school, or high school and how you and that friend or a few friends had such a tight bond. You went to war for each other, you ate lunch together, you may have joined the same activities, or you shared your deepest darkest secrets. Friendship is a bond between the two individual people. The same way you trusted that best friend in your schooldays is the same trust you should have in your spouse, but higher confidence!

Nate took a very long time to ask me to be his girlfriend. Although we knew of each other, we didn't reliably know each other. He made sure that we were friends and that we genuinely liked each other and liked being around each other. Until this day, he is without a shadow of a doubt my best friend. We talk about everything, and we do everything together. He knows secrets, and I know secrets. We are two peas in a pod.

Let's take the time to focus on everything good about your partner. How are you both alike? Are your interest similar?

I call him my better half because at times when I want to think a certain way, he will give me a different perspective. He will reason with me and let me know when I'm wrong. That's what best friends do. They hold each other...a-ha...*accountable*. Best friends should be able to tell each other when they are wrong and give advice without it being a dispute.

From this day forward, you have an obligation to your spouse. Sadly, that is why most people don't get in relationships, let alone get married. They don't want the responsibility of another person, their feelings, their baggage, or the commitment in general. Obligation to your spouse shouldn't be looked at skeptically, with apprehension, or encumbrance. If you ever find yourself in considerable annoyance and second guessing with your significant other, I can almost guarantee you that is not the person for you.

At one point, I made a commitment to eat better and work out a minimum of thirty minutes a day. I slowly eased my way into the process. First, I started working out, still eating what I wanted. Then, I started eating healthy while still working out. It was a process. Now I'm up to sixty minutes a day, and my healthy eating habits have become superb.

However, it took some thought and willpower. Now I feel obligated to get to the gym every day and eat better because of the gratification I get. It took time and effort to get to that point, but I feel so much satisfaction in the gym sweating and seeing inches fall off my body.

The foundation in your relationship is where you will slowly get to the point of wanting that gratification of relationship prosperity. It's a process. You are getting to know each other and what each other likes and does not like. Then, you start getting better at it. You start understanding your partner, their past, and why they act the way they do. Next, you fall completely in love with this person and want nothing but peace, love, and joy with them.

At that point, you obligated yourself to be the best you can be for your significant other. You obligated yourself to support their dreams and ambitions, empower them, and uplift them in their shortcomings. When you love someone, and when you are ready to get married, the obligation to your spouse is pleasurable and achievable.

From this day forward activates longevity. In your vows, you did not say, "from this day forward until...." You said, "from this day forward." There is no timeframe or limit on forward. Your forward may be ten years, twenty years, fifty years, or more; however, the length should not be determined on emotions, but it should be determined on death. Just because you have an emotion of anger today doesn't mean you'll have the anger tomorrow. If you base your timeframe on emotions, you'll be on the emotional rollercoaster for the rest of your life. If you base it on any emotion, let it be the emotion of interest to make it until death.

Are you prepared for longevity?

If you aren't prepared for longevity or maybe you are anxious about it, I am going to equip you with my three favorite qualities to ensure longevity. After nearly thirteen years of marriage, I made it over the "newlywed blues." I've made it through the toughest thing we have ever had to go through yet, and I made it through all the other pointless arguments that led to nothing.

Forgiveness will ensure longevity. *Let it go*! Don't harp on what can't be changed. Don't beat a dead horse. Don't allow the temptations of the devil to distract you from prospering in your marriage vows. Notice Matthew 18:21-22 KJV, "then came Peter to him, and said, Lord, how oft shall my brother sin against me, and I forgive him? till seven times? Jesus saith unto him, I say not unto thee, Until seven times: but, Until seventy times seven." Jesus was not telling us only to forgive 490 times, but endlessly. Lack of forgiveness will only harden your heart and hurt your relationship. Know that there is peace, love, and hope in forgiveness.

Patience will guarantee longevity. You will grow every single day with your partner and with development, patience will be needed. Not only will you and your partner grow as people, but you will grow annoyed with things your partner does and says. Romans 12:12 KJV says, "rejoicing in hope; patient in tribulation; continuing instant in prayer." If there weren't any troubles in life, the Bible would not instruct us to be patient in tribulation. God has plans for us and our marriage. If we lack patience with our partner, we lack patience with God and trust that he will get us over whatever mountain we are trying to climb.

Being hopeful will most definitely assure longevity. Nothing good will come from a negative mind. Always remain positive and optimistic through every situation. Most of the time, when you want something, you will do what it takes to get it. You have to want your relationship to succeed. When you genuinely want your relationship to succeed, you will be able to remain optimistic through the low valleys.

If you have full confidence in the Lord, you should have complete confidence that he won't put any more on you than you can bear. You should have hope in his word when it tells you to put all your cares and concerns on him because he cares for you (1 Peter 5:7 KJV). Remember that every low valley that your marriage gets in is preparing you for something.

Are there any low points in your relationship right now? Where can you forgive, show patience, and be hopeful in your relationship? If not, think about the long-term and how you can invoke these components to ensure longevity.

Vow Triumph

In marriage, you can't plan for every little detail that will happen; because we don't know. What you can plan for is to be the best you can be. You can plan to give it your best shot knowing ahead that you will be faced with difficulty. You can plan to find forgiveness in mistakes, patience in growth as a couple, and hopefulness when things look doubtful.

Reflection Notes

_____

_____

_____

_____

_____

_____

_____

_____

_____

_____

_____

_____

_____

_____

_____

_____

_____

For Better Or Worse

Come on people! If marriage were effortless, minimalist, or with no trouble, do you really think there would be a worse part in your vows? Don't be surprised when worse comes. You've been warned, and yes, I said *when*. The misconception is worse won't happen. The mistake is thoughts of people thinking they are exempt from marital challenges.

Misconceptions are often warranted by unrealistic expectations of marriage. Review the reasonability of your marital expectations.

Better days differ among the person and the couple. What you think may be better days may not be better days for me. However, one commonality in relationships is that better days always exist directly in the beginning. I like to call them the days where things were simple. It consists of those beginning stages where you ignore every flaw of your significant other because the relationship is fresh.

I look back at me and my husband's better days, and I think about how we were traveling, having romantic date nights, spontaneous outings, and just downright fun. We didn't have a care in the world. I felt like we were sitting on top of the world—just the two of us.

We all should know what better days feel like. It would be extraneous to acknowledge how awesome it is to have good days as we all know how to manage those. You manage those by continuing to evolve individually and as a couple, relying on your foundation principles, and honoring your relationship.

When faced with adversity, always remember your better days and the promise of what will come in the end.

Do you remember when you were young? Did you feel untouchable and invincible? I'm guilty! I remember one time in middle school I had stayed out all night in Atlantic City, New Jersey with my friends. *Middle school! Can you believe that?* As I age, I realize how moronic that was. Anything could have happened to us that night. We could have been raped or abducted. Naturally when you are young, you don't grasp the fact that things can happen to you.

Nonetheless, when I got married at eighteen, I carried that same untouchable attitude in my marriage. *Marriage is a piece of cake! I got this down pat! I know what I'm doing!* In my little undeveloped head, I thought every day would be incredible and perfect. As a grown woman, I realize my thinking was overly optimistic, which turned into an unrealistic expectation of perfection.

I didn't realize that marital problems existed at the time. I didn't know what a trial and tribulation looked like, and I didn't know that matters come up to challenge you in marriage. I didn't realize that bad days accompanied good days. I didn't know that merging two people as one would take patience and fortitude. I didn't know what I was truly getting myself into. I was just a young unwise girl who knew she was in love. I soon found out when life hit me.

Reflect on the maintenance needed to preserve a car. To keep it running, you should get your oil changed, rotate your tires, get the filter changed, and change the breaks periodically to name a few. All these activities are maintenance done on the car to prepare it for the hardships of the road, the craters, a possible long drive, and protection of your engine.

List some things you can do to properly fuel your relationship.

Marriage requires the same maintenance. It requires continually putting energy into the relationship and application of what we know and learn to uphold our marriage. Prepare for anything to happen in your relationship as your relationship is not invincible to the growing pains all couples are met with. When you are prepared for what's to come, it will limit the failure process and ease the struggle. Be encouraged that there is maintenance that can be done to prepare you for upcoming challenges that will be faced.

Keep your foundation intact so when you are feeling substandard you are armed and prepared to battle. Retaining a strong foundation consists primarily of knowing where each other stands on all matters of life. Once you are married, there should be no confusion about what you both want or don't want.

However, it is understandable that people change. Communicating concerns, anxieties, and thoughts is the maintenance in preventing confusion down the line, and always being aware of what your partner is feeling. Continuously talking about life goals and the logistics of life should never get monotonous.

Nate and I have always established how we want to raise our children. Recently in a casual conversation I said to him, "I want the kids to know how to budget early on." Discussions like this are not formal, but they are informative. He is still being made aware of what we previously talked about and is aware of where I stand on the matter. He is aware that this is important to me. Should he object, the door is open for a conversation to work through it.

If you aren't consistent with expressing life concerns, start each week with a couple's meeting on life.

There is significance in continuing to date your spouse even after you are married and especially when children get involved. One thing I was informed about was that having children changes the dynamic of your relationship. Take your time having children after marriage, enjoy each other's company, and don't allow anyone to pressure you.

Taking alone time to date one another will continue success in your friendship foundation, increase your communication, help you to unwind through the tough days, and most importantly keep that beginning spark going. Life can happen and time moves so fast the older you get. Having these moments of intimacy is critical.

This is the part of relationship maintenance where you need to put energy into your relationship. Put some fresh oil in your car! Date nights don't have to be elaborate and expensive. The alone time where you are connecting, having an open dialogue, and enjoying the presence of one another is extravagant enough. You find out a lot about a person just through transparent conversation.

Nate and I had the best date night's ever when we were impoverished. We had no money to do anything but stay in the house. Karaoke was a frequent activity amongst us in our home. The infamous "contagious skit" was filmed at some very dark times of having little to nothing, but feeling blessed and content with everything. That everything was pure love and satisfaction of each other's company.

Plan a date night that demands you to spend little to no money and enjoy the chemistry between just the two of you.

Back in high school, I ran Track and Field. I wanted to condition myself for winter and spring track, so I decided to run cross country. Let me be the first to tell you that I was not a long-distance runner. It was a real challenge for me. I struggled severely keeping up with all the real long-distance runners. I was fatigued and even ready to quit at one point, but slow and steady always wins the race.

It is imperative to not monitor in an unhealthy way of what others have going on or how they are doing in life and in their relationship. Everybody's journey is made different and unique for them. I struggled because I was focused on keeping up with the other runners. I wasn't doing what works for me and I was failing.

By not quitting, sticking it out, making sure I went to practice every day and staying in my lane, I was able to obtain one cross country medal that season. That challenge made me stronger in the end, and it equipped me for winter and spring track and the next cross-country season.

Worse can bring challenges and test the strength of your relationship. Like me running cross country, your problems can make you feel like quitting and inferior to those succeeding around you. However, your challenges are a blessing. I often tell couples that I wouldn't want to have something that doesn't challenge me. I don't want a relationship where I'm not being challenged to be better.

When you are challenged, you are fertilizing growth. With growth comes experience. Embrace the challenges that you face in your relationship. When your strength is tested, two things will happen. One, you will come out stronger. Two, you will be equipped for future battles. With those two, you will always win in life.

What challenges have you been faced with thus far in your relationship? Identify one problem and think about how it made you stronger. Remember that challenge you overcame when you are faced with your next obstacle.

Worse is not just financial troubles, infidelity, or those major forces that cause friction. Worse can be the little things like bad attitudes, wanting to always be right, no communication, bottling up feelings, feeling inferior and isolated, name-calling, too much co-dependency, or lack of accountability. The little things can cause just as much tension as the big things if they aren't managed accurately.

Managing worse can seem challenging and exhausting. The truth is, it is if not done right and willingly. If you don't want to do something, it becomes tedious and will wear you out. You must freely and enthusiastically work at it with intention, purpose, and achievement in sight. You must be persistent, positive, and locked into the task. Don't ever take your eyes off the prize of triumph in your marriage. When you lose sight of the end goal, you lose focus on how to expertly complete the mission.

Consider something tough that you had to overcome. Maybe it was on the job or in life. Triumph didn't happen overnight. I'm sure you had to put in a tremendous amount of effort to get to the rewarding point. The same thing happens with marriage.

Remember when mama told us, "money doesn't grow on trees?" She was telling us we need to work for the money we get. Good marriages don't just fall out of the sky. They aren't born, but they are built. The successful marriages that you see are people that have chosen to put in the work to make it right and to make it work. There are ways to manage the worse part of your relationship, and I will tell you exactly what worked for me.

Don't be too proud to talk to other successful couples about how to manage worse in your relationship.

The Bible instructs us in 1 Thessalonians 5:17 KJV to pray without ceasing. Pray and pray again. Not just any prayer either, but the Lord's prayer. Nothing more and nothing less. In the seventh chapter of Matthew, the Lord taught us exactly how to pray and what to say.

My husband and I felt like that was all we needed to get through the days. God covered all our bases in the Lord's prayer. What is valuable is that you understand that prayer is a comforter. Prayer was designed to provide relief for the faint at heart, provide guidance for the lost, and clarification for those who need it. Prayer did just that. It comforted us.

Every morning at around 7 a.m., no matter where we were, we prayed. Praying together made us look at each other with compassion. Jesus is peace and brings peace. When you are reading your Bible or at church, most of the time you are in harmony and satisfaction. True peace began to fill our home. Instead of pointing the finger, it was accountability we were exercising. I noticed when we started praying together, the small things that got on my nerves didn't seem to bother me anymore. I saw that I was speaking with kindness. I noticed that I was not easily angered.

Active listening and excellent communication are essential in managing the worse in your relationship. I can admit I was the woman who thought my husband was a mind reader. Maybe if I stare at him hard enough, he will see precisely what's going on in my brain. Maybe if I roll my eyes, sigh loud, suck my teeth, or cross my arms, he will get the memorandum.

Although these are nonverbal textbook types of communication, they are unproductive in relaying meaningful information in a partnership such as a marriage. Nonverbal communication is not the right way to communicate in a marriage.

Where can your communication become more open? The next time you find yourself upset, take a minute and politely express your feelings.

I had a thing where we would be in the car, and I would say to my husband, "I could go for some Chick Fil A" as we were driving by the restaurant. I would immediately get frustrated because he wouldn't stop. My words should have been, "I want some Chick Fil A; pull over!" I had an expectation of him knowing exactly what I want without me having to tell him.

When communication does happen, always be clear and effective in your expression. Be transparent about what it is you are trying to convey. You are the only person who knows your true feelings. You are the only person who can identify what your problem is. You can't be mad at someone because you think they should know something, and you can't be angry at someone for not being able to interpret your miscommunication.

Along with me not being clear, my approach was sometimes all wrong. Often how you approach someone can affect the reception of your communication as well. People are more accepting when you have a softened approach.

I learned to communicate better as the years went on. I learned that a "soft answer turns away wrath: but grievous words stir up anger" (Proverbs 15:1 KJV). Meaning, your tone and your response to communication will be the deciding factor of what happens next. If you speak with respect, you will get respect. If you speak with deference, you will get healthy communication and resolution.

Don't be afraid to call a time out from a potential acrimonious conversation. It's better to walk away and take a breather than to engage in what you could later regret.

Active listening is where managing the worse can become exhausting. I'll be frank. It takes practice, skill, and if you don't truly value your relationship, this won't work. It doesn't just come to you one day. I am still mastering the art of it till this very day. Active listening is more about listening to what the person is saying as opposed to listening to respond. Active listening is removing the thoughts inside your head and focusing on the details of what is trying to be expressed.

As a young wife, it was tough for me not to listen to reply. When you are young, all you hear is yourself. You are the only right person, and you think you see the bigger picture. Marriage is a team. You and your spouse are a team. On the basketball court, if the point guard calls out a play, it's the other team members job to listen to the play. If the team members think it should be another way, it will cause confusion. The goal is to come to a consensus together. Active listening won't work unless you do.

As a spouse or future spouse, recognize that you should be working together and not against each other. Recognize that communication is vital in deciding life decisions. Recognize that communication is essential in managing the bad days of your relationship. Silent treatments are momentary solutions whereas excellent communication will produce permanent and healthy resolution.

I loved running Track in high school. No matter how hard the practices were, I was coming back every day and every year for four years to perfect what I loved to do. Love is the most powerful feature you can have in your relationship to manage worse.

You must believe you are with the right person. Many people have disorder in their relationship because they are mismatched. They are not with the right person. They are fighting for a relationship that is not intended to be long-term but meant to be a lesson. Trials and tribulations are normal in a relationship, but chaos is not.

Love is going to be willing to work with you and not against you. Love is going to conceal your flaws and faults with acceptance and consideration. Love is going to understand that you are imperfect but perfect at the same time. Love is greater than any mistake made, any annoyance, and any shortcoming.

When my husband and I came out of our worse stages—the stages I call the "growing pains," we both realized something indispensable. What we realized when the worse part was over was, it wasn't material things that made us have better days, it was our love for one another.

My husband always said that during those times, he had hope because he thought we were going to be blessed abnormally in the future, talking about financially. He said that after we came out of the struggle united, he realized what we had in each other was the abnormal blessing. It was *true* love.

There is triumph in a struggle, blessings that you will witness, and lessons that you will learn.

Reflection Notes

_____

For Richer Or Poorer

Finances are one of the top causes of tension in a marriage and have been said to lead to many divorces across the world. Although it is not the number one cause of divorce, it has the potential to ruin everything you have built and will continue to develop. Because of the severity of finances, this is the reason why your foundation must be stable and that you must be rooted in true love.

Finances have a way of consuming energy, time, your mental state, overall wellbeing, everything. It is draining and leaves you feeling full of hopelessness and impossibility. The constant worrying of where money will come from to pay this bill or where money will come from to eat will take a toll on any solid relationship. It is all you think about; leaving little room to focus on building and keeping a positive and healthy relationship.

We learn in biblical teachings that we will leave this world with what we came in with...nothing. The overall health of

your relationship is more important than your wealth of finances.

Many people wonder how someone could end up in financial distress, especially if you have never been there. There are a plethora of reasons why people end up in financial trouble. It could be misappropriating funds, bad budgeting skills, lack of income, employment issues, or perhaps life happens.

Whatever the cause, often the result is the same. That includes a range of emotions from anger, to frustration, to aggravation, and back down to unhappiness. I have felt all these emotions and these emotions felt me. These are the emotions that left me in severe depression. At the time, these feelings left me numb and wondering what I ever did so wrong to deserve this.

Let's be truthful! Whether you are married or not, nobody wants to be broke. Not everyone wants to be rich, but nobody sits around and says, "today, I want to be broke." It just doesn't happen that way. Should you happen to know a person who thinks otherwise, please send them to me. I would love to talk to them! As a result of that thinking, nobody ever thinks "for poorer" will happen in their relationship, especially if you are already established and feel you have it going on.

My husband and I were in this same predicament. We had it going on, and you couldn't tell us anything. I was in the military, and he was making good money at a prominent limousine company in Princeton. It was the best! We lived and acted humbly, but we did enjoy the fruits of our labor by taking vacations and having spontaneous outings.

While you are dating, one element you should monitor in your relationship is your partner's spending habits. It's acceptable for a person to want to treat themselves. The problem is when the person goes overboard not thinking about the future and what *could* happen in the future.

It's never too early to discuss logistics like financial stability in your relationship. Even after marriage, always continue the conversation.

The big word is *could*. Good or bad, anything is possible. You may be up today, but down tomorrow. It is imperative that you have a budget or plan in place. If your partner has poor spending habits, most of the time it will lead to unnecessary financial stress.

On the contrary, having a partner with money is great. It's marvelous! The only mistake we as people make is striving to find a partner with money. As much as we don't want to struggle financially, I want you to understand that money is not everything.

The truth is you should prefer to have a partner who is more emotionally stable than economically stable. Remember how I told you anything could happen? We went from money to broke in the same year. If we weren't emotionally stable for one another, we would have never made it through richer or poorer. Emotional stability is what will get you to the end.

Is your love strong enough to handle financial stress?
What can you do to ensure that it is sturdy to withstand?

My husband and I hit severe financial stress mid-2008. We were in a dilemma and stepped out on faith. After a job offer was rescinded right before we were about to move, we had to make a tough decision. Together, we decided to continue our journey to Georgia from New Jersey. We had been to Georgia, applied to our apartment, and paid rent for the month. As we felt like we were too deep in, we figured it wouldn't take long to find jobs. *Boy, were we wrong.* That one decision was the beginning of a life-altering change that I believe God put us through for a reason.

Decision-making was something that I took for granted. I never really had to put much thought behind decisions because I was young with no real-life situations to make crucial decisions. What had I ever experienced? Deciding to break up with a knucklehead boyfriend at thirteen? *How relevant!*

I would later learn to look at every component of decisions, even the hard parts. The parts that you don't want to see are the hardest to face. You want to see the good in everything; however, you have to remain realistic of the possibilities of all angles.

Because we were young, we didn't look at the "what if we don't find jobs soon enough?" We looked at it how young people look at everything, matter of fact and oblivious. That one decision we made as young adults affected the rest of our lives. We didn't think we would deplete our savings and money we already had before we found jobs. We didn't think about the future.

Make decisions with full thought of everything possible that could go wrong.

We were a young couple who went from having financial freedom to being bound and burdensome with financial stress. Not only were we suffering from the loss of our brand-new car, but we were suffering from other significant damages. Our financial downhill consisted of our gas being cut off, which prevented us from cooking the little bit of food we did have.

Because of the gas, we had to settle for the dollar menu at various restaurants. We could only eat one time a day. Wendy's crispy chicken sandwich was a frequent favorite. It is something I still order today as a humbling reminder of where I came from and what we went through as a couple. When we were big balling with a few extra cents, we went over to the Sonic to order off their value menu.

I never will forget one time in particular where things became extremely hard for us. There was no food in the house and no gas. We had a few dollars left and barely hanging on. To eat, we had to share one crispy chicken sandwich, which we split right down the middle.

It was one of the most humbling moments of my life. Hungry, annoyed, and fragile, we sat at the table and thankfully ate what we had. I never knew what real hunger felt like until that day. Sometimes it brings tears to my eyes thinking about that day. It is something that I can distinctively remember as if it were yesterday.

When I tell you we have been through everything financially, I genuinely mean it. I remember in November 2008 because we hadn't paid our car note in a very long time, our black Durango was repossessed. Thankfully, we had another car that was completely paid for.

Nonetheless, the sting and violation we felt of having something that we worked for taken away was enough to put us both in a state of desolation. The valuable lesson on this now that I look back is although you may suffer a loss of something or may not get something you desire, focus and be thankful on what you already have because God may make you lose that too.

Read about Paul in Philippians 4:11 and how he learned to be content.

The most interesting part about our time being impecunious was the fact we had no cable. It's funny to me because today we have no cable, but by choice. Times were a little different then. Netflix, Hulu, Fire Stick, and others weren't prevalent or either they weren't existent.

We relied on ourselves to pass the times and our love for DVD movies like *ATL*, *Meet the Browns*, and *Four Brothers* became instant replays. I resonated with *Meet The Browns* so much because I felt her story as my own. The ending of the story was comforting, hopeful, and relevant to what we were going through.

What intangible characteristics do you possess in your relationship that you think will help you in coping should you have to endure financial distress?

Let this be an example of one of my foundational principles of friendship. Sitting in the house with no job, no cable, and no money can frustrate a person. The toll financial stress takes on you alone is intense, but not working and no promising job leads are even more overwhelming. There is room for arguments, misunderstandings, low blows, and the blame game when you have time to sit around and think about it. We had nothing but time.

Friends have a link, a bond, and a connection with one another. They enjoy the company of each other and the closeness. If you aren't friends, you won't be able to make it through rough patches. Real friendship will allow you to be of support instead of being discouraging. Real friendship will enable you to understand instead of pointing the finger. Real friendship will allow you to have nothing yet feel like you have everything.

Months went by, and Nate started to work a little small job that wasn't paying much. In our minds, it was better than nothing. We needed all we could get. I wasn't complaining about the little income we did have. I counted it all joy (James 1:2 KJV).

With one car left and short on money, we did what we thought was right. We had to survive, and we were law-abiding citizens who wouldn't do anything to jeopardize our integrity or character. So, we went and got a title loan; which was another poor decision that would later have a trickle effect.

If you are familiar with a title loan, you understand that it is a complete setup for failure and if you don't have enough money to pay it off in time, you are screwed. We fell into the trap and couldn't pay the loan, and they took the car away in the fishiest way possible—at the dealership, but that's a story for another time. I had become so angry with my husband around this time. I had this 2002 Saturn that I paid for with my money at a young age, which I was so proud of, and it was gone.

Naturally when you are going through any adversity in a relationship, how you handle the situation will make or break your relationship. If you manage it with regret, blame, and spitefulness, your relationship will start to resemble that. There will be confusion, resentment, and all the unhealthy affects you don't want in your relationship.

Coping with the loss of my car taught me a few things. I don't want to define myself by what I have or don't have, my possessions are not worth peace in my relationship, materialistic things can be replaced, but true love doesn't come by often.

One of two things is going to happen when you go through relationship struggles. You either falter, or you maintain. You either want to forfeit, or you want to stick around for triumph. Think about people who make the President's list in college. They didn't get that award without studying and applying themselves. They didn't get that award by standing around and waiting for something to happen. They got the award through determination, hard work, and dedication. Your relationship struggles are similar. To abide and make it to triumph, you are going to have to put something into the relationship to get something out.

Choose to abide through the hardships of your relationship.

After all we went through, the struggle was not finished. We had one more hurdle to cross, and that was losing our apartment to become homeless and having to live in nasty motels. We journeyed to three of them. The first one was dreadful, but that second one was where God allowed me to utilize strength and positivity to make it.

The image of the room was as a room in a movie where hookers go with their "johns." The stench of the room smelled like pure death and the bathrooms were unbearable. As the room was so small of a space, our clothes carried the smell of death within them. Wherever we went, I was reminded through my clothes of everything we were going through.

What we endured as far as having no cable and not being connected to the world, going without gas at times, and having limited food was our training. To gain strength, you must go through some training. Training can sometimes be intense and tiresome, but it is worth it in the end.

The training is building resistance to withstand the test and get the results you were hoping for. In a relationship, the result is to make it out successfully and unscathed. That's what happened to us. The stress of cars being repossessed and the limited food trained us to be more resistant. It prepared us to be strong while sleeping in those horrid motels.

One piece of knowledge I gained in our financial struggle was respect for the durability of our relationship. You will be surprised at what you can endure if you try. Millennials typically don't stick around to reap the benefits of success. So, let me tell you what sticking around did for me to encourage you. It made my relationship stronger. Our foundation was solid from the beginning, so I didn't think it could get any stronger. Nevertheless, it did!

We became strong in the sense of togetherness, being unbreakable, and firm in our decision to love each other no matter what. Nothing was coming or could come to shake it or tear it down. When you build a firm foundation in the beginning of your relationship, the storms that later come won't easily move your foundation.

It also made our relationship healthier. During that time, we learned patience with one another. We learned how to communicate our thoughts and feelings effectively. We learned to control our emotions. We learned that we are allowed good days and bad days. We learned to adapt to change. We learned to grow with one another instead of against each other.

Finally, it made our relationship meaningful. The whole time we were looking to be saved from financial stress, but during that time we didn't realize we already possessed the powerful asset I described earlier of true love. It was all we needed to make it. After going through all that, we realized we have a good thing. We wouldn't have known if we hadn't of endured. Your relationship struggles are a gift if you stick around to open the present. The present of knowing that with God you can get through anything.

Don't always look to gain financially. Money will not buy you true happiness, success, love, faith, hope, and endurance. Money will not hold you at night when the world seems like it's caving in on you.

Having no money does not equate to hardships and having all the money in the world is not an exemption from difficulties. Some millionaires struggle every single day internally. The outside shimmers, but their insides are just as dim as a blacked-out television.

Write or think about a list of five things that you love about your relationship that have nothing to do with money.

It's easy to look back and say what you could have done differently and what you should have done differently. It's easy to judge someone when you haven't been in someone's circumstances or experienced the choices they had to make.

I'm often asked would I do things differently and I always say no. God gave us this path for a reason.

Don't look back on your struggles and wish to do things differently. Look back on your struggles and be thankful you made it. Look back and be grateful that you were chosen to endure and be a source of strength to other people going through trials. Look back with gratitude of your own personal testimony of the goodness of God.

It took years and years to recover from the financial hole. Suffering from repossessions and having little income resorted in buying cars from the buy here, pay here dealerships. This is another lesson of making sure when you make decisions, you look at the whole picture and not part of it. Make sure you understand that there are effects to the choices you make.

Before you make any life altering decisions, utilize a pro and con list to help with your decisions.

There is always hope. Years later, I would be able to look back and be thankful when we were able to walk into a dealership with a loan we got from a bank and pick out the exact car we wanted. Years later, I would be thankful that we can eat in five-star restaurants. Years later, I would be grateful that I was able to understand all the good that came out of it. There is no real lesson if you don't see all the good that came from your hardships.

If you stick it out through richer or poorer, you too will see that there is hope. Nothing worth having comes overnight. Every struggle, battle, and feeling of exhaustion will give you the experience and wisdom to know the difference between valuable and the invaluable. Be strong enough to withstand and know from my story that God has a divine plan for your life.

Create a robust financial plan that includes a regular savings.

Angela E. Rolle

Reflection Notes

In Sickness & In Health

Machado Joseph Disease is an incurable genetic disease similar and can be confused with Parkinson's disease. Symptoms include memory loss, speech issues, clumsiness, trouble swallowing, which all leads to paralysis. It's progressively being researched, and there is still an abundant amount of information to learn.

Regardless, this disease is a nightmare that looms over my husband. His family on his father's side suffers from this daunting and debilitating disease. Because of the severity, my husband has witnessed several of his Uncles and his Grandmother pass away.

Since the disease is genetic and his father has a mild case of it, there is a 50% chance that one of his kids already have it. We have learned and accepted the fact that there is a strong possibility that my husband is the one with the disease.

As a wife, it's tough to look at him and his potential and see what could happen. It's hard to think that he could end up in a wheelchair unable to lift his arms to feed himself or be confined to a bed. I understand entirely why he doesn't like to waste time and why he always wants to seize the day. From what he has experienced since a child, life is short.

Sickness can happen to anyone at any given moment. No one person is exempt from that. Whether you are living in the known or the unknown of illness, it behooves us to appreciate the invaluable lesson of living in laughter and love. Tit for tat, being unreasonable, aggression, and arguments are all irrelevant. Learning to let go of the things we can't control in life and the small meaningless matters we bicker and banter over are influential in living in harmony, love, and mirth.

There are signs that my husband shows of possibly having the disease, but I like to contribute them to him just getting old. It is an often conversation we have about getting the genetic testing, but I don't press the issue. I understand his wishes of what's the point in knowing if he has the disease. It won't change anything except be on his mind every single day as he looks at his family and knows what is about to happen. I'm sympathetic in knowing he would rather prepare for the worse and expect the best in the end.

Are you prepared for if sickness happens in your marriage? How will you manage it?

Dealing with a sickness of any kind should be treated with altruism. It's not just the big sicknesses that we have to worry about, but everyday illness like the flu, common cold, or maybe just not feeling well.

The worldly joke is when a man gets sick, he is on his death bed; but when a woman gets sick, she must continue with the daily routine. Oddly enough, I find this to be true. Statistics show that women who get sick as opposed to men are more likely to end up in divorce. Women are typically expected to do more and carry on as if they don't ache or need a break.

Empathy deals with understanding other people's feelings and being able to put yourself in their shoes. We have all been sick before, and we all know how it feels. We all have been to a point where all we could do was lie around and drink fluids, if that.

As a significant other, you should automatically feel empathy for your partner since you both are now one flesh. Therefore, picking up the necessary slack should become natural. If someone is sick, go the extra mile. It shouldn't feel burdensome. Collaboration is a part of any relationship and marriage. Without it, there is no victory, championship, or achievement.

A month before my husband and I were about to leave for Georgia, my grandfather was in a bad electrical fire where he was burned severely. He ended up in the hospital on a ventilator fighting for his life. As the primary breadwinner in the household, adjustments had to take place. He ended up not being able to return to work and was put on disability.

My grandmother couldn't point fingers or cry a river. She had to pick up the slack and do what was needed to maintain their home, finances, and livelihood. She implemented teamwork by realizing one half was down and out, so pity time needed to be over and survival mode needed to take place.

If you find yourself pointing blame at your partner, ask yourself what you can do to initiate change.

With sickness comes change. Change is something that is feared because most people love being in a comfortable and familiar space. If it isn't broke, we typically don't fix it. It's always good to change throughout the years to keep you abreast should things change by force.

When a person gets sick, finances will have to be adjusted which will entail a change. Responsibilities may weigh more substantial on the non-sick person who will have to adapt to change. This will require flexibility and moving out of your comfort zone. Change is ultimately good but can be harmful if you aren't familiar with it. It will test the limits of your relationship.

Think about an argument you had with your significant other. Even if you think about the most powerful argument, ask yourself did you stop loving that person. Think about a mistake your significant other made and ask yourself did you stop loving that person. No matter what that person did or didn't do, it didn't change the fact that you love them.

As such, sickness should not make you stop loving your partner. Love is not real when you can shut it on and off based on what someone says to you, what they do to you, or should they happen to get sick. Sickness is a condition that should be treated with unconditional love.

If your significant other were to get sick, can you truly love without condition? Ask yourself are you in love with the health of the person or the heart of the person.

Since I knew my husband's family as a child and was aware of their family ailment, absolute love made me look past the condition. Of course, it is worrisome to know someone I have a boundless love for could endure one of the most terrible genetic diseases I have ever encountered. It's hard seeing him stumble, have trouble remembering, or hesitate over words. Nevertheless, I am going to do what I vowed to do, and that's support, love without limits, and be accountable for what he can't adequately do.

The leaning tree is not always the first to fall. Your partner may get sick and be on their death bed, but God has a funny way of doing business. Throughout the Bible, you saw Christ healing people. Lazarus came back from the dead due to Christ working his wonders. Regardless of what Doctor's say, he can heal your partner from any sickness that may be obtained.

My all-time favorite writer, Maya Angelou said, "people will forget what you said, people will forget what you did, but they will never forget how you made them feel." In sickness and in health makes this statement so real and is a reminder to treat people as we want to be treated.

Monitor your "huff and puff" when your partner asks you to do something while sick.

What happens if your partner becomes healed and regains their full strength and you treated them poorly? They will remember how you made them feel. Did you bathe them when they needed it? Did you feed them if they couldn't lift a spoon to their mouth? Did you help them around the house because they couldn't move as quickly and efficiently as you?

Many times, sickness can be prevented. A conversation about why a person got sick and if they could have prevented it is not relevant once it happens. Patience when someone purposely harms their body is applicable in this situation. Everyone is combating some demon. It may be small, it may be big, and it may not look like yours, or be appropriate to you. Where there is an effect, there is a cause.

As you previously stated in your vows, you are accountable for this person. You should support them in their cause to help them fight the effect. Drug abuse could be looked at as something someone can control. However, if we could control our mistakes, we would never make them.

Although you may not have been hit with sickness, there is still preparation for it. Don't confuse negativity with preparing for the worse. Negativity is a state of mind where you think nothing is right or will go right. Preparing for the worse is like having an emergency fund. It's using your common sense to understand that, "stuff happens!" The groundwork of preparation includes working on developing your mind, body, and soul.

Get in the mindset of utilizing a savings plan. I can't stress enough the importance of planning financially for whatever comes up. Setting financial goals and savings can dim much stress should you become ill. If you are in a predicament like myself and Nate where you are living in the known of the unknown, it is undoubtedly significant that you establish financial restrictions. It may come a time where you will need to fall back on the money you have stashed away.

Protect your body. If you are willing to get genetic testing to know what you may be faced with in the future, do so. Get your physicals completed every year. Pap smears for women, and regular examinations for men and women are central in maintaining your health. There is a reason why insurance companies provide free physicals. It can find the problem before it starts or worsens.

Eating healthy plus regular exercise are also ways to protect your body. What we put in our bodies can impact major organs. If we aren't drinking enough water, it can cause kidney problems, fatigue, and headaches. These are things to think about when you love someone. Your body is your temple, and you should treat it as such.

There is no preparation that you can do with your soul because that was taken care of by Christ long ago. What we need to do as people is learn to accept God's will for whatever he has planned for us and our partner's life. The fact is we don't know when time will be no more. We don't know what the future holds for us. All we can do is study our Bible and be equipped with the word of God to fight whatever weapon that is formed against us.

Saying the vows "in sickness and in health" is truly an act of mystery. When we get married, we don't know what will come. We don't know if we will live the rest of our lives together in health or in sickness. Suitably, this vow shows kindness, humility, integrity, strength, passion, and most importantly unconditional love.

Vow Triumph

Appreciate your moments of living in good health and love one another while you are still able and coherent. If sickness should rise, remember the vow that you said before God. Remember you got married with the intent to love without confines and with grace and mercy.

Mercy is forgiveness shown towards someone. Where in your relationship can you have mercy on your significant other?

Angela E. Rolle

Reflection Notes

_____

_____

_____

_____

_____

_____

_____

_____

_____

_____

_____

_____

_____

_____

_____

_____

Till Death Do Us Part

So much happens between when you get married and death. So much that can deter you or so much that can determine your strength. Remember your wedding day and how happy you were or will be. It doesn't matter if you had a big wedding, a small wedding, or if you went to the justice of the peace. Hold on to that day because you will need it to get over the impediments that all relationships go through.

The only way to get through marital frustrations is through communication.

There are ups and downs, trials and tribulations, positivity and negativity that happens. No one is excused from experiencing burdens. There will be times you may feel like mentally checking out. There will be times where you may want to walk out the door. There will be times where frustration will build over every good feeling you have.

Death is the timeframe for parting from marriage. It's not when you get tired of being in the union. It's not when you get annoyed with your partner. It's not when your partner makes a mistake. It's not when you don't get your way. It's until one of you passes away and never to return. That means through all the good and bad you must be able to endure.

You can't run a long-distance race without having the right amount of endurance. Runners didn't start off being able to run long distance. They had to build on that. They built their endurance slowly through training, running long but slow, and then having the proper diet to sustain their stamina.

Marriage is like running a long race. The only difference is the competition isn't against another opponent; it's against you. Self-endurance is required in your marriage to make it until death. Running the race with diligence will define if you get to the ending or not.

The competition is against what you are equipped to handle and how well prepared you are to finish the race. Are you hydrated with patience? Are you strengthened in love? Are you trained to climb the hills? When you sweat and feel exhausted, are you remembering why you started in the first place?

What are you going to do to ensure you finish the race out?

I remember when I was a young wife, I thought I had it all figured out. I thought this way because growing up I saw what a wife looked like on the outside. I saw the tangible as far as cooking, cleaning, and taking care of the man to make sure he has all he needs. What I lacked was the intangible. I lacked the knowledge required to endure marriage and the strength to equip me for the race.

Many times, we don't succeed at something because we lack information or training. A student who doesn't take notes in class, read their books, or ask for help won't succeed because they lack information and they lack properly utilizing their resources and tools. To succeed in relationships, you must feel indebted to learn all you can to be successful and understand your role.

Acceptance and accepting each other as you are is the first step to enduring until death. You won't go through the marital journey together without misunderstandings. Your partner won't do everything correct. Your partner will make endless mistakes. Your partner will have ways about them that you may want to change or become frustrated with.

One thing for sure is so will you. We all want forgiveness when we have mishaps. We all want to be respected and valued for our opinions. We all want to grow as an individual with someone right there ready to stimulate the greatness within us. What we want is mercy, respect of differences, and a partner invested in us. This constitutes acceptance and will aid you in prospering.

There is a disclaimer! Don't misconstrue approval for acceptance. Approval is an endorsement, and an endorsement is support of the action. There are certain behaviors that you may let slide that will create consent for your partner. Infractions such as physical abuse, emotional abuse, intertwining other parties in the bedroom, demands, or infidelity are all activities that require acceptance from a distance and are not healthy in the relationship.

Accepting behaviors such as lack of cleanliness, lack of urgency, laziness, assertiveness, or even things uncontrollable like memory issues are mercy and require patience to work through. Understand the difference and make a conscious and healthy decision to decide if you are going to approve or accept.

It is necessary to realize that you won't go through life agreeing on everything. As two separate individuals, compromise is imperative in making it until death do you part. Compromise can seem unreasonable for a young couple or for someone who thinks they are more intelligent than others.

To fully execute compromise, you must be willing to grow. Growth is opening your mind and thoughts to new ideas, opportunities, and plans. There may be a more rational approach to executing a problem. Your partner may have more experience than you; but if you are congested in your way or the highway, you won't be open to seeing the better idea. Remember, your way is not always the way. With compromise in your relationship, it will create healthy development and openness.

Be honest within and ask where you lack compromise in your relationship. Ask God that he opens your mind to change that.

Compromise was not in my vocabulary as a young wife. I wasn't trying to negotiate anything. I knew what I knew. It was immaturity that made me miss wanting to grow and expand new ways of thinking and doing things. I wasn't looking for a solution to a problem. I was looking for agreement with my statement, which never works out. Your choices and actions once you get married don't just affect you, but they affect your partner as well. The Bible says the twain becomes one flesh for a reason.

There is hope and encouragement in compromise. If you ask any veteran couple, they will tell you the older you get; the more nonchalant your mind gets about small matters. Your compromise is a lot healthier and more impactful. It's not that it's unimportant or pointless to you. You are just more aware of picking and choosing the right battles to fight.

When my husband and I were dating, I still had exes that I called friends. I knew I wasn't a cheater, so in my head it was harmless. What changed my perspective of having certain friends of the opposite sex was an incident that happened a few years ago. The lightbulb came on, and I realized that you might have respect for something, but that doesn't mean someone else will.

An ex that was returning home from the penitentiary contacted me via Facebook, and I accepted his friend request. Keep in mind it was an ex from the eighth grade. In my head, it wasn't that serious to begin with; however, it was that serious to him.

He started talking extremely reckless after finding out that I was married, and insinuating that he would harm my husband. He had no respect for me, my husband, nor my marriage. In my head, there was no way we could ever continue to be friends. So, I gave him a "blessing" and blocked him. This is not the only incident I've had with an ex threatening my relationship, but it is the first incident as a married woman.

The point of it all is you can have the best intentions in the world. You can know your limits and that you can withhold. That's great; however, the problem lies with the other party. Sometimes your respect for your relationship won't always match someone else's respect—especially if they are trying to make a move and have little morals.

The problem also lies with you allowing the disrespect and you keeping the disrespect surrounded by you. Don't give people a permit to disrespect your marriage. Most importantly, make sure that you are respecting and honoring your marriage in front of and not in front of your significant other. People will only respect what they see you respecting. People will only honor what they see you honor.

Infidelity is one of the top causes of why people don't make it until death. Lack of boundaries in your relationship is the most legitimate reason why. Setting healthy boundaries for friendships of the opposite sex, more specifically exes or people you may have had intercourse with is beneficial to the health of your relationship. Keep yourself away from people who are unhappy with themselves and who are unhappy in their own relationships.

When having friends of the opposite sex, reflect on the nature of the relationship and how it will influence your current relationship.

I've abandoned the temptation of infidelity by not even putting myself in the position to commit the deception. After sixteen years of being with my husband and thirteen years of marriage, it has never crossed my mind to commit infidelity or look at another man with lust. When you appreciate what you have and love what you have, there is no looking elsewhere because nobody else will look as good.

News flash! It's not always right on the other side. Everything that looks good does not always taste good. Remember at the family cookout how delightful the potato salad looks, but when you eat it, it has no flavor, or it's watery? Don't lose what good you have at home tasting potato salad that looks beautiful on the outside, but on the inside has no integrity, self-worth, and lacks true love for you.

Plant the seed in your garden to produce your own nice grass and beautiful flowers.

I always ask couples, "what is more important?" Is your relationship with your significant other important or your relationships with the opposite sex? Focus on you and your partner solely. Think about that as you are setting boundaries.

Most importantly, respect your partner's opinions about it. Men are typically more naïve than women. Women can spot a homewrecker from miles away, whereas men don't recognize it. As a result, your partner may see something that blinds you; so it benefits you to listen, watch, and pray.

I remember being a kid and feeling as though time was stagnant. You remember the days, right? The days seemed prolonged, and adulthood was so far away. I wanted to rush time so badly to be grown. *If only I could go back*! When I became an adult, time became inverse. It started moving extremely fast. I looked up one day, and I was a thirty-year-old woman with so much life lived, and experience gained. I had a time frame on what I wanted and when I wanted it in my life. I thought I would at least have three kids by now and a few degrees under my belt.

"To everything there is a season, and a time to every purpose under the heaven:" (Ecclesiastes 3:1 KJV). Timing is noteworthy in making it until the end. There are lessons that you will need to learn individually and as a couple that will take time.

Think back on a time where you realized the lesson after it happened, and how it helped you at that given moment.

Some things may happen in your relationship that you won't understand right when it happens, but answers will be given with time. My husband and I didn't understand the cause of our financial stress when we were going through it. With time it was revealed to us the meaning and the story behind it.

Just like there is a time to weep, a time mourn, or a time to laugh, there is a time to understand. Understand that everything will make sense when God reveals it to you to make sense. The small hurdle that you were trying to jump over as a couple in the beginning may be a setup for a big hurdle coming down later on in life.

Know that everything that happens in your life as a couple will happen for a reason. There is a blessing in every lesson you learn. If you don't wait the time out, you will never get to the understanding part, the clarity, the "a-ha" moment of "that's why we had to endure this."

Have you had any relationship "a-ha" moments? How have they helped you work through matters?

Until death do us part is long-term and should be affiliated in your mind as pursuing longevity. Get in marriage with the idea of no matter what, I vowed to stay until death do us part. I promised to be accepting of my partner. I promised to compromise with negotiation where required. I vowed to remain loyal and committed to this one

Vow Triumph

person. I vowed with comprehension that with time everything will work out for good.

Write down a list of long-term goals you want to accomplish with your partner together as a couple. Where do you see yourself in the future as a couple?

Reflection Notes

According To God's Holy Ordinance

If you think you can live without God, you can operate without God, you don't need his guidance, or you have all the answers, this chapter is probably not for you. God's word is a requisite.

An ordinance is like a government. It's a rule, decree, direction, order, and command. God's ordinance is HIS holy word. These principles and practices were instituted for function and order. Notice how complex situations get when we try to handle situations ourselves. Notice how lost we seem to be when we aren't actively reading scripture and connecting with Christ.

There is nothing new under the sun, and everything we will ever experience was written in the Bible. My husband often says, "the Bible was not written for our entertainment; it was written to guide us through life."

Start off reading a daily scripture to connect more with Christ. Then up your daily devotion each month.

Instruction in the Bible is there to guide us through the daily trials and tribulations of life. Reading the Bible and adhering to the guidance within is the best practice we can do in life. Jesus told the Sadducees in Matthew 22:29 KJV, "ye do err, not knowing the scriptures." We, as people, are at fault not knowing the scripture. We are mistaken when we don't look to God from where all our help comes from. We are misguided when we think we have all the answers and all the power within our own hands.

God's ordinance on the sanctity of marriage was very clear and concise—love one another, honor, and respect your marriage. The scripture says in Hebrews 13:4 KJV, "marriage is honourable in all." Being boyfriend and girlfriend and even becoming engaged is excellent. As a couple, you should still respect one another. However, when you get married, you are entering a sacred covenant and promise to each other to work through everything and honor your commitment as husband and wife. It's a prestigious promise.

Wake up every day remembering the promise you made to honor your significant other and your marriage.

Honor happens with integrity. Integrity doesn't just consist of honesty, but your moral compass. Morality comes from knowing and understanding the word of God and what says the Lord. Until reality hits that we can do nothing without the Lord, we will never be fully equipped to live life the right way.

Integrity and honoring your vows is meaning what you say and saying what you mean. When challenges arise in your relationship, remember that you stood before God and your significant other and vowed that you would endure until death do you part. Holding on to that word is your integrity.

Realize that God's word is perfect and marvelous in our eyes. It's the only real source we need to sustain something as meaningful as marriage. Staying away from him and his word will only deter our progression individually and in our relationship. Counsel and advisement on marriage are throughout the Bible. There are a few things I want you to remember about God's word and what it says.

Isaiah 40:8 KJV says, "the grass withereth, the flower fadeth: but the word of our God shall stand for ever." When all else fails, God's word is still going to be held up, available, and relevant. When mother and father are gone, and friends disappear, you will find solace in God's word. The word that never fades will be readily available instructing you to love one another as Christ loved us. It will teach you that love is greater than any obstacle that may come in your path.

Love is limitless.

One thing that I got right as a young wife was comprehending that love covers a multitude of faults. I understood that love is greater than defects. I wasn't looking for the perfect person that had everything together. I wanted the perfect person for me. I wanted the person that would see beyond my imperfections and silly quirks. The person that would be willing to grow with me instead of against me. The person that would accept me as I am.

When you seem lost and conflicted in your marriage, utilize the scripture for discernment. Don't use worldly advice to navigate through tough times. The world doesn't contain the wisdom that is packed in the Bible. Use the word of God which is sharper than anything as your shield and defense against conflict. Hebrews 4:12 KJV says, "for the word of God is quick, and powerful, sharper than any twoedged sword, piercing even to the dividing asunder of soul and spirit, and of the joints and marrow, and is a discerner of the thoughts and intents of the heart."

One huge mistake I made was involving individual family members in my marital business. Involving family members in your personal affairs is a huge no. Let me tell you what happens when the family gets involved. When you are over a situation that you were mad about and included them in, the family is still going to be upset. Certain family members know how to move on from a situation, but you will have the overbearing ones and the ones that think they know everything in your ear yacking.

There is a reason why family and friends have a high percentage of influence on divorce. I understand that everyone needs someone to talk to, but discernment of our family and friends and the conversations we have are crucial to the success of the marriage. Talk to God as he is the only one able to bear all our burdens.

The next time your spouse gets on your nerves, don't call anyone. Talk to the Lord and read the word.

"But he answered and said, It is written, Man shall not live by bread alone, but by every word that proceedeth out of the mouth of God" (Matthew 4:4 KJV). The Bible did not say some of the words. It said every word. When God instructs the woman on how to be a wife and instructs the man on how to be a husband, sincere adherence to it will only benefit us in the end. We create a problem when we don't obey the word or think the other way is a little better. God is not like a man. He won't ever give us impractical guidance.

Job was a man that lived by God's word, and he was blessed tremendously for it. One day, God allowed Satan to come in and take everything away from Job. The blessed part about it was although everything like his substance and kids was taken away from him, Job still trusted in God. He always believed and lived by every word that God said. When his friends and his wife tried to sway him, he still lived by the word of God. What happened in the end? God blessed him with double of everything he previously had.

We need to resemble this in our marriage. God's word can sometimes sting, which is why some people tend to pick out portions that are relevant for them or leave certain parts of the scripture out. We want to justify our behavior instead of rectifying the behavior. A wife may have a hard time accepting submission, but the word was put in place for a reason, and we need to make sure we are doing our part by living by it.

We aren't perfect. So, where can you be more proactive in living by the word of God in your life and your marriage?

The Bible tells us that Satan has a desire to sift us like wheat. Satan loves to see destruction, especially amongst the children of God. He loves to see us flustered and see our marriage fail. He loves when we are fighting and arguing about nothing. Utilizing the word of God as the source of your strength on the path of marriage is a must. Psalms 119:105 says, "thy word is a lamp unto my feet, and a light unto my path." Walk with the word of God. Follow in the footsteps that God left for us. You can't fight the devil by yourself. You must resist the devil with what you know, and that's Christ.

It took me a while to realize that I can't make the marital journey by myself. I need the help of the Lord to get me through the rough days. I need the help of the Lord to guide my decisions and actions. I need the holy word to light my path when it gets dark.

At one point, I was ready to leave my husband right in Georgia and walk away from the financial struggle. It was God through his word that showed me, "you will reap if you faint not." It was God who instructed me that "all things work together for good." It was God who led me to scripture and fighting the devil with his word. He gave me that, and the knowledge to know there is reassurance and power in his name.

My hope for you is that you believe the report (Isaiah 53:1 KJV). Are you going to believe everything written? Are you going to believe God's word? Most importantly, are you going to use it in your marriage? Are you going to abide under the almighty so he can protect your marriage?

I was not able to make it over the mountains of marriage and get through the days of adversity without one thing— being powered by God. Since we don't have power on our own, it must come from the Lord. When you have the power of God behind you, you already have enough to equip you for the hardships. When you have the power of God behind you, high mountains seem low. When you have the power of God, you can be a force to be reckoned with.

Study the word of God every single day as power from God only comes that way.

Angela E. Rolle

Reflection Notes

154

I Pledge Thee My Faith & Myself To You

_____

We pledge all the time in our everyday life. As children, we pledged allegiance in the classroom, and we pledged to keep our best friend's secrets. As adults, we pledge to make our car note, mortgage payment, and credit card bill. A pledge is a solemn promise and our marriage vows are a promise of what we will do until death comes for one or the other.

Pledging your faith to your significant other is promising your partner that you will be trustworthy and reliable. True faith in your marriage is putting full confidence and belief in your significant other and your union.

You can't pledge faith and life to someone or something you don't believe in. If you don't believe a car is worth $25,000, you more than likely will find a cheaper car as you are not going to commit to that note. You can't pledge faith or life to someone or something you are not dedicated to. If someone tells you a secret and they're not your best friend, you may feel a little looser on the lips. Marriage is the same way. You must believe and be 100% dedicated to the cause. The only way to keep the binding agreement is by authentic love and knowing how to create a long-lasting love.

One of my secrets to a lasting relationship is getting self out of the way. It all starts with you and your selflessness. Those vows weren't about you. They were about your partner and what you are going to do for them and give to the relationship. Yes, you are pledging yourself and faith to your spouse; however, the action is to your spouse. What are you going to give to your spouse as opposed to what is your spouse going to give to you?

Getting married and pledging yourself to your significant other is a self-sacrificing act. If you aren't careful, it can turn into a selfish act. The "I" in marriage was not meant for what you want and need, it was meant for what your partner will want and need. *I* am going to love you in sickness and in health. *I* am going to love you for richer or poorer. *I* am going to make sacrifices for the advancement of our relationship. *I* am going to work through difficulties. *I* am going to give my all.

Where can you remove selfishness from your relationship?

Once we remove our self out the way and what we could possibly get from the relationship, we can truly focus on the wants and needs of our partner. Now, your partner should be matching you as well to make it an even playing field. However, I want to be clear that you shouldn't look at your partner and what they aren't doing. Look at yourself. Remember, it's about what you are giving. Be accountable for what you are doing, and they should be doing likewise.

My husband and I were extremely young when we got together and when we got married. Majority of our issues earlier on came from "I" and what *I* want. Lack of maturity played a major role. I was unable to get myself out the way and focus on his needs and wants, and my requirements as a wife. All I saw was what he wasn't doing. When you look at everything a person isn't doing, you miss everything right they are doing. You don't appreciate what they are bringing to the table.

Giving yourself to someone is one of those things that seems so authoritative. I shouldn't have to give myself to anyone; but on that day, you become a part of someone else and they become a part of you. There is light in giving yourself to your significant other.

A physical connection is trivial because eventually physicality won't be as consistent. When physicality decreases, you will need another connection to link you two. Think about giving yourself to your significant other emotionally. Holding yourself back and all you can give is not conducive to longevity and making your love prosper. Emotional connections are one of the most needed characteristics of a relationship. This includes all emotions, good and bad.

Vulnerability is the biggest emotion a relationship needs. Your partner should find refuge in you. When troubles arise in this world, you should be your partner's on earth go to person. Vulnerability exposes your partners weaknesses and allots for a candid dialogue of feelings that shouldn't be given to anyone else.

Is vulnerability present in your relationship? If not, what are you lacking to prevent it from existing?

My last corporate job was the most terrible experience of my life. It was like nothing I had experienced before. I had a manager who didn't like me, and the feeling was reciprocated. The manager was conniving and making it completely impossible to want to be there even though I loved being around my co-workers.

I was so unhappy there that it started to trickle over into my home. I would call my husband crying throughout the day saying I couldn't take it, and I would come home tremendously angry. The last several months I was there became an everyday crying session of discontent. Even though my husband has never worked in the corporate field and couldn't feel what I was going through, the refuge he built in our relationship foundation allowed me to be vulnerable.

Vulnerability needs to be created in your relationship. It starts with trust. Trust is built in many ways; but the most important two ways are with sincerity and through your actions. Words that don't match your actions are meaningless and actions followed up with negative words are condescending.

Vulnerability also needs to be maintained. Remember what I tell you and vulnerability won't be an issue in your relationship. Don't bring up the past. If your significant other confides in you about something, leave it where it is. Trusting that your significant other will not bring up your possible hurtful past will ease the creation of an emotional connection. Don't be judgmental. It takes a lot for someone to divulge personal information. Trust is lost where judgment dwells.

Fear plays a major role in willingly giving yourself to someone. People who have been hurt in the past have a hard time accepting someone good. They have a hard time connecting with someone out of fear of failure and being hurt again. God did not give us the spirit of fear. Don't allow fear to rule your life. Fear of the unknown is a natural emotion because we are human, but it shouldn't hinder you from moving forward in your relationship. When you are with the right person, your fear should decline as you become comfortable with your partner and the allowance of vulnerability is created. Live in confidence instead of fear.

What are your fears about marriage?

The pledge also contains aligning your priorities. Prioritizing what's important versus what is not important is defining what is most meaningful to you. It is defining what makes you set something or someone above something or someone else.

When we were going through financial struggles, we had to prioritize where money was allocated. The concern wasn't cable because what would be the point if we didn't have a roof over our head. It was more meaningful for us to have a home to go to as opposed to having cable.

Your relationship should be prioritized above all other relationships other than your relationship with Christ. Without prioritization, you can't fully pledge with the intent to keep the promise. Your prioritization to your significant other requires attention and focus. Like an infant needing its mother is how our partner needs us. In order to withstand the bad storms that arise and keep the grass green, relationships need devotion, attention, and enrichment.

How can you prioritize your significant other and the relationship? First, keep your significant other's needs and wants important to you. Remember that if it is important to your spouse, it should hold the same amount of standing to you. People typically want to feel that you are in their corner and that you understand them. That's part of being in a relationship—understanding your partner's needs and placing them first.

Where in your relationship can you prioritize better?

Also, don't be reluctant to embrace change. At times we fear prioritization because it will require us to move out of our comfort zone. It will require us to focus more on an uncomfortable situation as opposed to something that comes so natural and easy to us. When we are brought with a challenge, two things will happen. It will either be met with fear or confidence.

The best relationships have communication that is not always a positive. Meaning, the communication is not always something you want to hear. When your significant other brings a concern to you or addresses something that you are doing wrong, a change must be made to rectify the concern. Many times, we negate the concern because we don't want to change, it may be hard to change, or it may be hard to acknowledge your wrongdoing.

Marriage is the beautiful intertwinement of two individuals. The truth is not everyone will experience a good marriage. This is due to lack of action, commitment, and integrity it takes to withstand. Many times, the experience is often taken for granted and mistreated. Give yourself freely to your husband or wife and let God work out the rest. Always live in the moment, forgive easily, and remember that through your ups and downs, there is victory in your marriage.

Can you pledge to action, commitment, and integrity in your marriage?

***R**eflection* Notes

Epilogue

In the beginning, your love is close to perfect. This is because you don't see the transgressions of your partner, challenges seem minimal, and everything they do is right before your eyes. It's kind of like how my husband and I met and started dating. As time swiftly moves, you will find that transgressions become annoyances and challenges seem impossible to conquer.

It is extremely important that you learn to utilize your tools and resources to manage those challenges. At one point I was ready to walk away from my marriage because I felt as though I was too weak to handle the struggles God placed before us. What I now realize is I wasn't weak; I just wasn't properly equipped. I wasn't relying on the word of God to guide and direct me.

I realized walking away from the situation we were in meant walking away from my husband, and I was not willing to do that. My love for my husband allowed me to stay through the hardships of our financial situation and lack of maturity. When you find true love, no matter what comes up, you too will be able to stand firm against the tests you will be confronted with.

One of the greatest things you can possess on earth is finding true love in the person you love and adore. True love and being with your soulmate does not mean you won't have setbacks and failures in life. We were promised trials and tribulations. We were informed that "weeping may endure for a night, but joy cometh in the morning (Psalms 30:5 KJV).

I want you to understand that you won't get to the joy of marriage without enduring a little test. To endure you must stay until the end. The joy of marriage is all the lessons you learn individually and as a couple. I tell people all the time that my marital struggles allowed me to become rich. I'm rich in wisdom, experience, and knowledge.

Strength is something that I didn't know I possessed in the earlier stages of my marriage. Had I frivolously walked out I would have never been able to reap the benefits of what I have now, which is a precious and sturdy marriage. My faith was tested, and my marriage was tested. I feel so unworthy for all the blessings I am receiving in my life because I understand the state I was in. I remember feeling like all hope was lost and how weak my flesh got.

I learned through my marital struggles to fully put my trust in the Lord. The biggest blessing that came from all of this is my strong faith in Christ. What I witnessed in my marriage was miracle after miracle. God parted red seas for us. Although I had physical sight, I was spiritually blinded; he gave me sight. He healed me from the infirmity of depression. He met me at the road of Damascus to inform me of what he had in store for me next. For that, I am forever grateful of every struggle I had to endure.

Marriage is something that should be entered with consideration and thought. Through my transparency of me being a young wife and us going through financial stress, I hope that you found encouragement and guidance. I hope that you think fully about your vows and what they truly mean before you enter marriage, before you file for divorce, or when trouble arises.

All marriages have low points. You are not alone. Although your low point may not be my low point, believe that you can get through it, believe that in the end your marriage is worth it, and trust that there is triumph in your vows!

"Two are better than one; because they have a good reward for their labour. For if they fall, the one will lift up his fellow: but woe to him that is alone when he falleth; for he hath not another to help him up. Again, if two lie together, then they have heat: but how can one be warm alone? And if one prevail against him, two shall withstand him; and a threefold cord is not quickly broken."

Ecclesiastes 4:9-12 KJV

About The Author

Mrs. Angela E. Rolle is a motivational speaker and author. She holds a Business Management degree with further educational pursuance in Organizational Leadership. She is a graduate of the Chattahoochee Technical College Student Leadership Academy and has also completed many different leadership conferences learning different tools to becoming an effective leader. She is a proud inducted member of the National Society of Leadership & Success.

Rolle is a Silver member of Black Speaker's Network where she is focused on developing as a professional speaker. She has a love for writing and sharing her story of triumph in trying times. She had the pleasure of writing an article for *Elephant Journal* on how your beginning doesn't have to be your ending. This is the motto that she lives by. She is currently working with different magazines and websites to have more of her work published.

A United States Air Force veteran, she is tough but lovable. She is a visionary and wholeheartedly believes in serving others before self. Born and raised in New Jersey (South Jersey as she likes to point out), she learned the importance of business and leadership at a very young age. Rolle has five sisters with all her sisters having boy children, whom she loves and adores. She loves reading, writing, traveling, church, spending time with her husband, and taking a good nap on her spare time. Married at the tender age of eighteen, Rolle had to endure many failures and setbacks.

Thirteen years later and still happily married, she is the founder of Love Inspiry, LLC. She is a co-host alongside her husband of international podcast Love Inspiry. It has been listened in places like Indonesia, Canada, and India. Rolle is also the face behind Love Inspiry YouTube Channel and has many other upcoming projects on the way. She is a nurturing and straightforward God-fearing woman, wife, sister, daughter, granddaughter, and friend. Visit www.loveinspiry.com for more on her services.

.

www.ingramcontent.com/pod-product-compliance
Lightning Source LLC
LaVergne TN
LVHW011330080426
835513LV00006B/268